THE JOB-HUNTER'S
SURVIVAL GUIDE

Other Books by Richard N. Bolles

What Color Is Your Parachute? 2010 edition (9/1/09) revised annually

What Color Is Your Parachute? Job-Hunter's Workbook

How to Find Your Mission in Life

The Three Boxes of Life, and How to Get Out of Them

Books by Richard N. Bolles with Co-authors

Job-Hunting Online (5th Edition)
(Mark E. Bolles as co-author)

The Career Counselor's Handbook (2nd Edition)
(Howard Figler as co-author)

Job-Hunting for the So-Called Handicapped
(Dale Brown as co-author)

What Color Is Your Parachute? for Teens
(Carol Christen, with Jean M. Blomquist, as co-authors)

What Color Is Your Parachute? for Retirement
(John E. Nelson as co-author)

FIRST EDITION 2010

The Job-Hunter's SURVIVAL GUIDE

How to Find Hope and Rewarding Work, Even When "There Are No Jobs"

Richard N. Bolles
author of WHAT COLOR IS YOUR PARACHUTE?

Ten Speed Press
Berkeley

Copyright © 2009 by Richard N. Bolles

Published in the United States by Ten Speed Press, an imprint of the Crown Publishing Group, a division of Random House, Inc., New York.
www.crownpublishing.com
www.tenspeed.com

Ten Speed Press and the Ten Speed Press colophon are registered trademarks of Random House, Inc.

Library of Congress Cataloging-in-Publication Data

Bolles, Richard Nelson.
  The job-hunter's survival guide : how to find hope and rewarding work even when "there are no jobs" / by Richard N. Bolles. — 1st ed.
      p. cm.
  Includes index.
  Summary: "An emergency, essentials-only guide to finding a job—even your dream job—in a challenging economic climate, from the author of classic career guide What Color Is Your Parachute?"—Provided by publisher.
  ISBN 978-1-58008-026-2
1. Job hunting. 2. Job hunting—United States. I. Title.
  HF5382.7.B628 2010
  650.14—dc22

                                2009019820

ISBN 978-1-58008-026-2

Printed in the United States of America on recycled paper 30% PCW

Design by Betsy Stromberg

10 9 8 7 6 5 4 3 2 1

First Edition

Contents

About This Book

I FIRST CONCEIVED THE IDEA of this book in February, three months ago. The annual editions of my perennial best-seller, *What Color Is Your Parachute?*, continue to hit the bookstores every September, but I felt there was also a need for a much shorter, less expensive book to help job-hunters who were hanging on the ropes during this brutal Recession. So I proposed a 100-page book at a meeting with my publisher back in February, and they said they could get it out by mid-July.

I quickly discarded the notion of simply copying portions from the big book, and decided to write this from scratch. "If I were job-hunting tomorrow," I asked myself, "what would be the most important things for me to know?" I wrote the book accordingly. In this, I had help. Every three months I conduct a workshop for five days in my home, to which come people from all over the world; I listen a lot. I learn a lot from them.

The most essential stuff is in here. Lots of other things aren't. No detailed treatment of shyness, or other handicaps, no lengthy discussion of interviewing or salary negotiation; they're all still in the main book. Here, we have to travel more swiftly.

A word of thanks to the folks over at the editorial department of Ten Speed Press in Berkeley, California:

Aaron Wehner, Lisa Westmoreland, and Betsy Stromberg, who labored mightily to bring this book out so quickly. Also much gratitude to Jenny Frost, head of the Crown Publishing division of Random House, who are the new owners of Ten Speed Press; she has been immensely encouraging. And a word of great, great gratitude to Phil Wood, founder and former owner of Ten Speed, my friend and publisher since the annual revisions of *Parachute* first began, some forty years ago. And 10,000,000 copies ago. I owe him a debt I can never repay. It was he who first proposed "a little book." I think that was ten years ago. (I'm slow.)

Now, a word or two about this book. I wrote it in the same style I always have written *Parachute*, namely, I write as I speak. I use italics, pauses, numbers, words, and spaces between paragraphs in inconsistent ways throughout, to convey the weight I intend for sentences, or the speed with which a particular sentence is read. In other words, I break rules, in order to serve a higher purpose: easy reading.

The Internet dominates this little book. Four of out five adults in the U.S. have access to the Internet, now, making old ways of job-hunting obsolete. If you're on the Internet, and if you're up to date on browsers, you know you often don't need the old **http://www** prefix before a url. So, I give you the bare citing necessary for a browser (in most cases) to know immediately where to take you. If that *doesn't* work, call up Google on your screen, and put the citing I give you into the search box on your browser, and I'm sure it will turn up the correct url for the site you are looking for.

Full Disclosure: I have my own website, **jobhunters bible.com**. I have my own email address, **RNB25@aol .com**. I am on LinkedIn, and Plaxo, but not Facebook nor MySpace. My call. I have enough to do, as it is. I twitter once or twice a week (ParachuteGuy). I spend about two hours a day online. No more than that. I like to write, plus I have a lovely wife, Marci, and a useful life, and I like to get out in the sun. After all, I live in California.

—Dick Bolles
May 12, 2009

Preface

A PARABLE ABOUT STUPIDITY. *A bunch of people were in a rowboat, after their ship had to be abandoned. Suddenly, they noticed, with quiet alarm, that one man was using a drill to make a hole in the bottom of the boat beneath his seat. As the water was beginning to come in, he looked up and said, "Don't be alarmed. I'm only drilling under my own seat."*

How did this world get into the economic mess it's currently in? Well, to speak in glittering generalities, far too many of us (*both individuals and nations*) spent too much, borrowed too much, lived too high, saved too little, invested with too much risk, and played a Ponzi scheme with Nature. And when all this came crashing down, the consequences affected not just ourselves, but others around the world. And thus we learned that if you create a global economy, as we have in this Age of the Internet, you end up with all of us being in the same boat. And now what any of us decides to do, has consequences for others and not just ourselves. We see it even in metaphor: if I default on my mortgage, it lowers the value of all my neighbors' homes.

Currently the world is going through a dreadful shudder, as it sobers up to what it has done, and sees the need to reform its economic ways. We may call the shudder "hard times," or "recession" or even the big D word. The name doesn't matter. It amounts to a gigantic economic hangover that is worldwide.

And so, consumers have new goals now: as a group we are trying harder to pare down our debt, to depend less on our credit cards, to set aside more savings, to live within our means, and therefore to spend less. As a result, companies are downsizing, even going under, and millions of us are losing our jobs—however temporarily—not to mention our homes, our early retirement, and our dreams.

For many of us, unemployment is a new and sobering challenge. And sometimes we feel, frankly, lost. Even bewildered.

History reminds us that this too shall pass. Challenges, since America's pioneer days, have always been met, and conquered. It's just a matter of time. In the meantime, here is a survival guide, for these new uncharted seas.

It's not a magic bullet, and it won't solve all your problems. But I hope it helps; and gives you, most of all, both patience and hope.

—Dick Bolles
rnb25@aol.com
www.jobhuntersbible.com

1

There Are Always Jobs Out There

IF THERE WERE A TOWN that had only five jobs available in the entire town, and each job was filled and each person employed in those five was very happy with what they were doing, it might be safe to say, to some poor guy or gal out of work in that town, *There are no jobs out there*.

But if it were a town with 100 people who had jobs, that might not be so safe to say. Eventually, someone's gonna get sick, or move, or die. And then a vacancy will be created, that needs to be filled. With 100 jobs, there might be several such vacancies.

And if it were a town or city with 1,000 people who had jobs, or 10,000 or 100,000, there would be still more vacancies. For the principle is: the larger the workforce, the more certain it is that there are jobs out there—vacancies being constantly created due to human factors: people getting fed up, people getting promoted, people moving away, people falling sick for a long time, people retiring, people dying without warning, and so on. And in addition to vacancies, there are always inevitably new jobs being constantly created by invention and creativity, not to mention computer or technology advances.

The larger the number of people who have jobs, the more certain there are and will be job vacancies out there, waiting to be filled.

So, exactly how large is the number of people who have jobs in the U.S.? It is of course not 140, nor 1,400, nor 14,000, not even 14,000,000, but 140,000,000. That's one hundred and forty million. So, with promotion, moving, sickness, retirement or death, it follows that there are jobs out there falling vacant, and waiting to be filled. Always. That's just human nature.

How many jobs fall vacant? Some experts say it amounts, each month, to 1 percent of those who have jobs. Which in this case, would figure out to 1,400,000 vacancies per month currently.

Other experts, citing historical records for the period 1994–2004, say it in fact amounted to an average of 1,250,000 per month, year in and year out, for that period. That was the figure Ben Bernanke suggested, in an address he gave at Duke University back in 2004, before he was made Chairman of the Fed.

Well, I just saw in the news the April 2009 unemployment figures. They said that 13,200,000 people were unemployed but were officially looking for work, and 2,100,000 were unemployed but had given up looking, and then there were 9,000,000 part-time workers who want full-time jobs but can't find them. So, your figure of 1,250,000 monthly vacancies, doesn't come any-

where near matching the number of people who want to find work. It still sounds like an awful situation, wouldn't you say?

Absolutely. But this gap doesn't just exist during brutal times. There are always more people looking for jobs than can find them. That's why there are always at least 8,000,000 people who fail to find work in the U.S. even in the best of times. Job-hunting is all about competition. When any of us is out of work, in good times or bad, we always have to compete with others for any job that interests us.

It's just that in brutal economic times the competition grows a lot, lot more fierce; and people who have elementary job-hunting skills that were adequate enough to get them through easy times, now find those skills insufficient for the time at hand.

Still, even in this worst of economic times people are finding jobs, every day in the year. A recession or Depression wakes everybody up to the fact that they need greater job-hunting skills.

What do you mean by greater job-hunting skills?

Well, there are four pillars, I think:

1. Assume that finding work is *your* job. Don't wait for someone else to come and save you—the government, or anyone else. If you are someone with faith, the rule is simple: pray as though everything depended on God, and then work as though everything depended on You.

2. Be willing to work *hard* on your job-hunt. Don't just give it 'a lick and a promise,' and then give up. 'Working hard' means time and persistence. Lots and lots of time.

Days, weeks, months. And be smart in your use of time. Learn a lot during this period. Learn which job-hunting methods have the highest success rate, and which have the lowest. Invest your time accordingly.

3. Do a thorough and detailed inventory on yourself. You think you don't have time to do this? Oh yes you do. Incidentally, this step is more overlooked than any other I can think of, yet has more to do with a successful job-hunt than anything else I can think of. You will want to be focused—laser beam focused—during the time you are looking for work. You want to know, and you want to be able to describe to others, what you are looking for in the way of work, in the greatest detail. 'Staying loose' about what you're looking for is job-hunting suicide.

4. Learn everything you can about the job-hunt in 21st-century America. Go beyond what you learned back in high school, or—worse—out on the street.

   In brutal times, it's time to update your knowledge. For example, do you know the 18 different ways there are to look for work? Do you know how many of these you should use at any one time? Do you know what to do next, if the Internet and posting your resume doesn't turn up anything? And if you decide to use a resume, do you know what is the one criterion by which you should decide whether to include or omit any particular item? If you get a job-interview, do you know what is the time limit you should observe in answering any question? And finally, do you know the one question you should ask, in the interview, that will make a difference in whether you get offered the job, or not?

Remember above all else, in brutal economic times the familiar ways may not work. The ways that worked last time you were out of a job, may not work this time. Marshall Goldsmith famously said it: *What Got You Here, Won't Get You There*.

Be ready to observe, to learn, to change your way of doing things. Be ready to reinvent yourself, with a new identity. No longer, "I am an auto worker (*or whatever*)" but "I am a person who . . ."

Okay, but before we continue, I just want to register my distaste for the fact that the job-hunt is all about competition. I think that sucks. There has to be a better way.

I couldn't agree with you more. Cutthroat competition offends the spirit and the soul. I once got a glimpse of a better world. I was sitting on a bench in Walnut Creek, California, eating an ice cream cone. An old lady, with white hair, came and sat down beside me. "Isn't this a terrible time!" she said, by way of striking up conversation. "Yes," I agreed. "You know," she said, "there used to be a mine up in the hills over there. During the Depression everyone was out of work. My father heard that they were hiring, up at the mine. So he went up there and stood in a line outside the hiring shack. Since the wait was long, he struck up a conversation with the man behind him. Eventually, as the line moved, my father found himself next in line, outside the shack. When he went in, the hiring manager said, 'You're in luck. This is the last job I have to give out today.' My father turned and took a look out the door. 'In that case,' he said, 'why don't you give it to that man out there. He has four children depending on him, and I only have two. I'll find another job.'"

So, out of compassion, he gave away the job that was his.

If only we could replace competition with compassion, the job-hunt would be a better place. Not to mention the world.

P.S. The compassionate man, her father, found a job the following week.

Summary: Eventually we will come out of this. It will be over. It's only a matter of time.

What we need, in the meantime, is patience. And compassion.

2

How to Find Hope in the Midst of a Brutal Downturn

I REMEMBER AS VIVIDLY as though it were yesterday, the time I got laid off when I had a wife and four small children. My boss delivered the news just before noon. He mumbled the usual condolences. I stumbled outside, into the bright sunlight. It was lunch time in San Francisco, and as I wandered around the city dazed, I heard laughter, everywhere. I remember thinking a totally irrational thought: *How can you all be so happy? Don't you understand? I just lost my job. The whole city should be in mourning. Even the sun should be hiding behind the clouds today.*

Nobody seemed to care. They went about their business oblivious to the fact that my whole world had just collapsed. I wondered how I would tell my wife and kids that I didn't have a job anymore. I knew the news would make them anxious, and afraid. I guessed what their thoughts would be: What about their future? How long would it take me to find another job? Would we starve, in the meantime?

I had lost my job before, but I was single back then. Now I had five people depending on me. Their fate was in my hands.

If you think I knew what to do, you are out of your mind. I was a babe in the woods, so far as job-hunting was concerned. I did eventually find work. But it took me several months, and I made every mistake in the book, along the way.

Out of this experience, however, was born great sympathy. I think this happens to every person with any "character" who loses their job. You can never again look into the face of someone who has lost their job, without remembering, without feeling kinship and empathy, remembering how you felt when it was your time. You want to reach out to them. You want to give them a hug. You want to help them, in any way you can.

The world thinks of unemployment in terms of numbing statistics: thirteen million people out of work *here* (that was at the height of the Great Depression, and also is the current number in the U.S.). Twenty million people out of work *there* (that is the current situation in China, as I write). But I think of unemployment, now, in terms of faces—thirteen million sad or haunted faces, etched with fear, searching for hope.

I've been out looking for work, and I'm here to tell you, there are no jobs out there. Just how do you keep hope alive, during this brutal Recession?

It is simply not true that there are no jobs, out there, as we saw in the previous chapter. But that brings us then to your question: how do you keep Hope alive?

The answer is relatively simple:

The secret of keeping Hope alive is to always have alternatives.

For example, there are eighteen alternative ways of looking for work. They are:

1. **Self-Inventory.** Before you do anything else, do a thorough self-inventory of the transferable skills and interests that you most enjoy and do best, so you can define in stunning detail exactly the job(s) you would most like to have, to your family, friends, contacts, network, and employers. And then use this knowledge to focus your search for work.

2. **The Internet.** Use the Internet, to post your resume and/or to look for employers' "job-postings" (vacancies) on the employer's own website or elsewhere (Career-Builder, Yahoo/Hot Jobs, Monster, LinkedIn, etc.).

3. **Networking.** Ask friends, family, or people in the community for job-leads.

4. **School.** Ask a former professor or teacher for job-leads, or career/alumni services at schools that you attended (high school, trade schools, online schools, community college, college, or university).

5. **The Feds.** Go to the state/federal unemployment service, or to One-stop career centers (directory at **www.career onestop.org**).

6. **In Your State.** Go to private employment agencies (**www.usa.gov/Agencies/State_and_Territories.shtml**).

7. **Civil Service**. Take a civil service exam to compete for a government job (**http://federaljobs.net/exams.htm**).

8. **Newspapers**. Answer local "want-ads" (in newspapers, assuming your city or town still has a newspaper, online or otherwise). The Sunday editions usually prove most useful. (See **http://tinyurl.com/d58l8z** for how to use them; for a directory of their websites, see **www.news link.org**.)

9. **Journals**. Look at professional journals in your profession or field, and answer any ads there that intrigue you (**http://tinyurl.com/dlfsdz**).

10. **Temp Agencies**. Go to temp agencies (agencies that get you short-term contracts in places that need your time and skills temporarily) and see if they can place you, in one place after another, until some place says, "Could you stay on, permanently?" At the very least you'll pick up experience that you can later cite on your resume (**http://tinyurl.com/dxrdjy**).

11. **Pickups.** Go to places where employers pick up workers: well-known street corners in your town (ask around), or union halls, etc., in order to get short-term work, which may lead to more permanent work, eventually. For the time being, it may be yard work, or work that requires you to use your hands; but no job is too humble when you're desperate.

12. **Job Clubs.** Join or form a "job club," where you receive job leads and weekly emotional support. Check with your local chamber of commerce, and local churches, mosques, or synagogues. Excellent directory at Job-hunt .org (**http://tinyurl.com/7a9xbb**).

13. **Resumes.** Mail out resumes blindly to anyone and everyone, blanketing the area.

14. **Choose Places That Interest You.** Knock on doors of any employer, factory, store, organization, or office that interests you, whether they are known to have a vacancy or not.

15. **The Phone Book.** Use the index to your phone book's Yellow Pages, to identify 5–10 subjects, fields, or interests that intrigue you—that are located in the city or town where you are, or want to be, and then call or visit the organizations listed under these headings.

16. **Volunteering.** If you're okay financially for a spell, volunteer to work for nothing, short-term, at a place that interests you, whether or not they have a known vacancy, with the hope that down the line they may want to hire you (**www.volunteermatch.org** or **www .networkforgood.org/volunteer**).

17. **Work for Yourself.** Start your own small business, trade or service, after observing what your community lacks but needs (**http://tinyurl.com/yqt7pc**).

18. **Retraining.** Go back to school and get retrained for some other kind of occupation than the one you've been doing.

Now I give you a puzzle. Researchers discovered some years ago that the majority of all job-hunters simply *give up* by the second month of their job-hunt. They stop looking for work. Maybe they resume later; maybe not. But initially they give up, after a month. Why do you think that is?

Well, it turns out that it was and is related to whether or not they thought they had alternatives. In a study of

100 job-hunters who were using only one method to hunt for work, say the Internet, but had no alternative, typically 51 abandoned their search by the second month. That's more than half. Lesson from this: No alternative, bye-bye hope.

On the other hand, out of 100 job-hunters who were using more than one method to hunt for work, typically only 31 abandoned their search by the second month. Two-thirds of them felt they did have alternatives, so they kept right on looking for work. Lesson from this: When you have alternatives, you have hope. If one method doesn't work, that's okay; you can still try the other.

And in the case of job-hunting, as we saw, you have eighteen alternatives you can choose between.

Does this principle apply only to looking for work?

No, it applies to every situation you may be facing during this brutal economic downturn. Whatever your challenge, if you've adopted one strategy for dealing with that challenge, but it's slow to work and you're losing hope, save yourself from despair with this simple question: What alternative way is there of dealing with this problem?

And why stop with just one alternative? Debra Angel MacDougall, co-author of *6 Reasons Employers Say No* (Penguin Publishing, August 2009), recommends you find more than one alternative. She suggests you ask yourself: What are *two other ways* of dealing with this problem? (Whatever *this* problem is.)

In her many years of helping people in the U.S., Australia and Europe, particularly those who are down and out, she learned that people gain the most hope when there are three alternative strategies to choose between, rather than just two.

Why aren't two alternatives enough?

Debra found that people often just can't make up their mind, in choosing between two things. She found they freeze. But introducing a third alternative into the discussion breaks the logjam. She found it's easier for people to choose between three things, than to choose between two. Paradoxical. But there it is.

So, in facing *any* problem, challenge or crisis during difficult times, look for three alternatives, instead of just two. And do this every step along the way.

How to find those alternatives? When all else fails, try Thinking. And then ask others for ideas.

This importance of alternatives is particularly true when looking for work. Studies found that anything up to four alternative methods of job-hunting increases your chances of finding a job, and meaningful work.

Conclusion: It's probably going to be a long haul for you, this time out. Hope will sustain you along the way. You can do it, you can eventually conquer any challenge, given time. As long as you have Hope. Nurture it like a candle flame in a dark and wintry night, when the breeze is blowing. Keep that flame alive!

3

How Long Will I Be Out of Work?

I DROVE OVER TO THE SUPERMARKET, yesterday. I live in an East Bay suburb of San Francisco. The parking lot was full. It was hard to believe we are in a recession. Until I went inside the store. There, everywhere, were plastered signs headlined: "Unbelievable Sale"—on item after item after item. Four dollar stuff marked down to two dollars and change. That sort of thing. It was obvious that beneath the veneer of the full parking lot there was a lot of belt-tightening going on inside the store.

And that's because people are scared. According to the news yesterday, 70 percent of us are somewhat or very concerned that someone in our own household is going to be out of work within the next twelve months. So, 71 percent of us have cut back our spending on luxuries, and 41 percent of us have even cut back our spending on necessities.

We are "Scared." Or, if that's too strong a word, "anxious" at the very least. And with good reason. If you're out of work, these days, it might be only for a short time. On the other hand, it may be for a long time. Much longer than you think. The average (mean) length of unemployment now comes to 20.1 weeks, and climbing. Millions of people have been out of work longer than 27 weeks.

So, your unemployment could last twenty-one weeks or more. This means that if you're out of work, better be prepared for the long haul. Better to be safe, than sorry.

"Possibly twenty-one weeks or more" is very bad news for me. I'm in a precarious state financially, right now. Where can I go for help with my income and expenses?

First of all, let's talk about where not to go. You will find that if you use a computer or watch TV there are people anxious to help you when you're down and out. Or so they say. They use words like "Free" or "Cash advance" or "Help with your mortgage."

My advice for dealing with all these "offers"? If they say "Free," as for example on the coupon sites (below), that's fine, if you can download "the thing" immediately or just give them your snail-mail address. But if at any stage the word "free" is attached to a request for your credit card number, walk, run, no matter what they promise. Never pay cash in hope of greater riches later, and never, never give your credit card number to *anyone* making you an offer, via online, via TV, via the phone. Not even if they say, "You can cancel within thirty days." Don't believe it. The Internet is filled with horror stories of credit cards being charged month after month, without consent. Most of these people making these offers to you are out to make money, and become very rich, by preying on the gullible. Their credo is "A sucker is born every minute." All these scams—and there are more every day—remind me of a verse from the Bible: "Be clear-minded and alert. Your opponent . . . is prowling around like a roaring lion, looking for someone to devour."

Speaking of which, check out **www.RipOffReport.com**. Look up any company you're thinking of doing business with, to see what previous customers or clients have to say about them. The wallet you save will be your own.

Okay, but what can I do when I'm really desperate, and my income is dreadfully low?

Well, if you're not out of work yet, start right now living more simply. The key word is "frugal." You can go to your computer and type the word "frugal" into a search engine like Google. You're hungering for tips about how to cut your expenses? You'll find hundreds of them, on the various sites that come up, such as **www.alwaysfrugal.com**. Naturally, this is a good thing to do if you're already out of work and have limited income or savings to tide you over the 20.1 weeks, or whatever.

To help cut your expenses, there also are coupon sites and "today only" sales sites. Coupons are not to be sneered at. They often are the way in which stores offer private sales (via the coupon discount). Among the sites that may interest you, are:

www.dealcatcher.com

www.retailmenot.com

www.clevermoms.com

www.couponmom.com

www.couponcabin.com

www.couponheaven.com

www.valpak.com/coupons/home

www.coupons.smartsource.com

www.fatwallet.com

www.thebudgetfashionista.com

Browse them, pick and choose the one(s) you like the best.

If you need to cut costs with particular items in your budget, put that item (e.g., "clothes") plus the word "budget" into your favorite search engine. For example, if you need or want to travel, and you're not yet down to your last dollar, try such sites as **www.budgettravel.com** or **www.wejustgotback.com**. Or, again, if you want to eat out, at a medium-priced restaurant, try **www.restaurant .com** where you'll find coupons that offer you a net of $7 off the cost of your lunch or a net of $15 off the cost of dinner, at various restaurants in your zip code.

If you decide you want to make up a budget for yourself, and you own your own computer (*which is to say, you're not just using the computer down at your local library*), you can go to **www.Intuitlabs.com**, click on "Personal Finances," and then download (for free) Quicken Online, and Quicken Picks.

Your overall financial goals? Well, that will depend on You. Most experts advise: live frugally, pay down your debt (most notably on your credit cards), and start saving, as much as you can.

What else is there, to help when I'm broke?

Unemployment Insurance

If you're out of work, sign up, if you are eligible, for unemployment insurance. You probably know what this is, but just in case you don't: these are cash benefits that run for a certain number of months while you are unemployed, and are available in the U.S. from your state government, so long as you regularly report in to them, on how your job-hunt is going. To learn how to apply, go to your computer (*or to a computer at your local library, if you don't personally own one*) and type the following two pieces of information into an Internet search engine such as Google: the name of your state, plus the words "unemployment insurance benefits." Once on site, look for the words "unemployment benefits." Or, simplify all this by going to **www.rileyguide .com/claims.html**. Free.

Greed being what it is, you may stumble across some website promising that for a fee they will help you file for unemployment benefits. You picture someone sitting down beside you, and helping you fill out the application form, line by line. And maybe showing you the secret of collecting some big bucks. Right? Unfortunately, their "help" is most likely just a booklet, for which they'll charge you around ten bucks, irrevocably ["We do not refund payment for any . . . reason"]—after they first get you to cough up all your personal information, on the pretext of tailoring their program to your special needs! All they will then do is send you or let you download that booklet [their "program"] telling you how to go file, yourself. And, let's not forget, they now have all that personal information you volunteered about yourself, to use for whatever purpose they choose. You can get the same help, and better, costing you absolutely nothing, by just using your Internet browser, as I described above.

Food Stamps

To see if you are eligible for this help go to **www.fns .usda.gov/fsp/applicant_recipients/10steps.htm**. This is from the U.S. Department of Agriculture, and is titled: "10 Steps to Help You Fill Your Grocery Bag Through the Food Stamp Program: Learn If You or Someone You Know Might Be Eligible for Food Stamps."

Health Insurance

Do you want it, when your expenses are tight? You bet you do. In any which way you can possibly afford it.

How do I find health insurance when I am sort of on my own?

Thanks to the Internet, there are several places you can turn to, for information and help:

1. **www.healthinsuranceinfo.net**. A site, maintained by the Georgetown Health Policy Institute. Chock full of information. Very comprehensive.

2. **www.ehealthinsurance.com**. It allows individuals to compare policies from different providers, and then purchase the one they like the best. It serves all states, except Maine, Massachusetts, North Dakota, Rhode Island, and Vermont.

3. **www.freelancersunion.org**. You need to work in one of the occupations served by this union; it is for independent workers or consultants. But browse the site, and see.

Even after all this, I'm still having a really hard time financially. I'm falling behind in paying my bills. I feel like I'm drowning. What can I do?

You have several choices:

a. Get a temporary job: one you cheerfully hate but it brings in money.

b. Get some financial counseling: to stretch what resources you do have.

c. Move back home temporarily: if your parents invite you to.

Let's start with the last choice, first.

Moving Back Home

This has long been a popular strategy for young adults just out of college, who can't find a job. But, people in their thirties, forties, or fifties are finding it may be a necessary strategy, when they're really down and out. Of course this won't work if you and your parents have never gotten along with each other, and when you were a teenager you couldn't wait to get out of there. Going back, at this later point in your life, would be an exercise in humiliation. Unless you love humiliation, look for any other way you can, to solve your financial problems. Maybe move in with friends. A marvelous couple once took me and my wife in, for a year, when we were hanging on the ropes, financially speaking, many years ago. It saved our life.

Assuming you have good relations with your parents, moving back home with them for a temporary period can be a financial lifesaver, as you pay what you can toward rent and food there, while you save as much as you can 'til you're back on your feet.

However, if you want my advice, don't just appear on your parents' doorstep, without any warning, begging to be taken in. Instead, first write or call and tell them in great detail what's going on in your life, *and just ask them if they have any advice.* Period. If they should think to offer you a room in their home for a temporary spell, while you get back on your feet, then for heaven's sake, take them up on their kind offer. If that happens, take great care to be an adult. Don't just "flop," and lie around all day. Pitch in, and help them with everything. And exercise the good old-fashioned virtue of gratitude. Think it. Say it. Out loud. Daily. Hourly. Thank you. *Thank you.*

Financial Counseling

Next strategy when you're strapped financially: get some financial counseling. You'll have to look around a bit, for this. It's easy to get bad counseling, from someone who thinks they are this big financial expert, but in actuality don't know what on earth they're talking about. You want good financial counseling. Ask around—at your church, synagogue or mosque, at your bank, at your local chamber of commerce, at any clubs or associations you belong to, and see if you can find a helpful soul who knows their business and can show you ways of paying off your bills steadily, if slowly; and who can show you how to make what little money you do have to spend, stretch further.

In general, their advice will most likely be: in this brutal economy, the priorities are frugal, debt, savings, spending—in that order. Live as simply as you can, pay down your debts, credit cards first (*and particularly the ones that are charging you the largest interest rate*). Then start building up your savings. Lastly, resume spending, buying those things you need the most.

A Stop-Gap Job

This is any job, I repeat *any* job, that will bring some money in. It doesn't matter if you hate the tasks you have to do, in fact it's better if you hate it. That way you won't linger long there. It's fine, so long as it brings in money, and allows you to continue looking for good-paying work which you would really enjoy.

To find a stop-gap job, look in the classified ads in your local newspaper or rag sheet at the supermarket, go inquire about any job that will stop up the gap between when you worked last, and when you work next.

Conclusion: I grew up during the Depression. There were five of us: Mom, Dad, my brother and sister and me. We had no car. My Dad took the bus to work. I never had any clothes that weren't hand-me-downs. (That was fine, except I remember one green suit that I particularly hated.) We ate very simply. We had meat once a week, pancakes and stuff like that for our main meal on other days. And the one thing I most remember: I never knew we were in a Depression. I thought everybody lived as we did. Our home was filled with laughter, and love. That was all I cared about. Living frugally is not the end of the world. It can give you room to notice what are the really important things in Life.

If you ever want to do further reading, see: Dave Ramsey, **The Total Money Makeover** *(revised and updated, 2007), Thomas Nelson, publishers. $24.99. In bookstores, online, or at your local library.*

    Also, **Suze Orman's 2009 Action Plan: Keeping Your Money Safe and Sound***, Spiegel and Grau, publishers. $9.99.*

4

The Best and Worst Ways to Look for a Job

WHEN I WAS IN HIGH SCHOOL, our daily gym class was an unending exercise in personal humiliation. Each afternoon that we went out on the field to choose baseball teams, I was always the last to be chosen. At which point the other team would declare, "You've got Bolles," and the team that was stuck with me would groan audibly.

I didn't blame them; frankly, I couldn't hit the broad side of a barn, when I threw. If I tried to throw to home plate, the ball usually ended up at third. I was awful.

The scene shifts, and I am now thirty years old. I am married, I am getting undressed at night, and I throw my dirty clothes in the general direction of the clothes hamper across the room—you know, one of those things that looks like a big rectangular wastebasket. The clothes go in the hamper, every time. I didn't notice at first; but when I did I thought, "What the . . . ? I'm supposed to be the worst thrower in the world!"

I watched carefully the next night or two, and compared what I saw versus my high school memories. That's when it struck me: back in high school, as the baseball left my hand I unconsciously closed my eyes—tight. I remembered this very vividly. By contrast, now I was throwing with my eyes wide open, keeping my gaze fixed on my target (the clothes hamper) all the way, until my throw landed there.

I was amused. I began a little experimentation each night, at bedtime. I focused my eyes not just on the hamper, but on *one corner* of the hamper; unerringly, from across the room the clothes went into the hamper, *at that corner*. I was entranced with my discovery that you have to keep your eyes on the target, and in some detail, because where your eyes go, there your throw will go! *Keeping your Vision focused on the target is everything.*

Soon after this, they had a National Driving Test on TV, and I missed only one question that night: "How do you stay in the center of your lane, on the highway?" I thought the answer was: *keep your eye on the lane divider on your side of the car*. But that apparently only causes your car to gently edge towards that divider. Turned out the right answer was: *by focusing your gaze fifty feet ahead, on the very center point of the lane*. I realized it was the same story that life was drumming into me, at this point: where your eyes go, there your car will go. *Keeping your Vision focused on the target is everything.*

Nice stories; but what does all this have to do with job-hunting?

Everything. I'll explain, but let's approach this in a kind of roundabout way. We saw in the previous chapter that to keep your Hopes up, over the long run, you need at least three alternative ways of looking for work. And on pages 9–11, we saw eighteen alternatives that you can choose those three from.

Naturally, you'd like a little more information about the track record of those eighteen, before you choose. You're suspicious that some of those alternatives might make worse use of your job-hunting time, than others. And you ask me:

Is that true?

Well, it depends.

It depends on where you live.

It depends on what kind of work you're looking for.

It depends on how hard you're willing to work at this.

It depends on how much time you're willing to spend on your job-search.

And, most of all, it depends on sheer dumb luck.

But generally speaking your suspicion is correct: over time, some job-hunting methods *are* consistently less effective than others. Some job-hunting alternatives do make better use of your time than others.

Unfortunately, there are no rigid comparative studies that would give you hard evidence for this. You just have to guess, and feel your way. Hard to do, if you're new to job-hunting. But if you've been in this field for forty years, as I have, and observed recession after recession, and good times after bad, you can make some really trustworthy guesses. Indeed, over the years, various studies have been done, here and there, and occasionally they come up with statistics that have guided me in these guesses.

So here are my impressions, for what they're worth; the five worst ways to use your time, followed by the five best ways to hunt for a job:

The Five Least Productive Ways to Hunt for a Job

#1: Success Rate: Only 7%

Mailing out resumes to employers on their own website or on job-boards, or by mail.

Method: You compose a piece of paper, or an electronic version of same, that is a summary or resume of your background and experience, and mail or post it on the Internet, hoping some bright-eyed employer will see it and invite you in for an interview.

Success Rate: This results in finding a job for 7 out of every 100 people who use this method. And I'm being generous in my guessing, here. One study suggested that only 1 out of 1,470 resumes actually results in a job. Another study put the figure even higher: one job offer for every 1,700 resumes floating around out there. The truth is, no one really knows anything except that the success rate is dismal. In the days before electronic resumes, I saw roomfuls of paper resumes 'on file' at some large employers. I thought of those rooms as 'resume tombs.' Now those 'tombs' sit on servers.

The Payoff for Using This Method: Works well if your resume is handed to an employer by a mutual friend, who highly recommends you. Works well if it strikes the fancy of an employer who is looking for someone with your skills and experience.

Biggest Problem with This Method: It is estimated that over forty million resumes are floating around out there in the cyberspace of the Internet, like lost ships on the Sargasso Sea. And in brutal economic times, there is a veritable blizzard of new electronic and paper resumes raining down on the heads of employers, from every direction, day after day. It's a bit overwhelming.

My Comment: Every job-hunter wants to believe in resumes. And their belief is that if well written, resumes *will* work, and get them a job. Consequently, there is a large army of 'resume-writers' in the land who are usually good sincere people; they make a decent living, helping job-hunters in every village and hamlet write a dynamite resume, for a fee, which can run up to a couple hundred bucks. Alternatively, putting "how to write a resume" into your favorite Internet search engine, like Google, will turn up loads of guidance, sometimes for free.

Of course, resumes do work—sometimes—or they would have died off long ago, like the dinosaurs in a parched and dreary land. But they remain a big fat gamble, and if your whole job-hunt is centered around your resume, you are liable to strike out, week after week, month after month.

By the way, employers often ask for your resume, if you contact them, or they promise to keep it if you've already sent it to them; novice job-hunters assume this means employers are really interested in them. Sometimes that's true. But sadly, it's also a standard response that many employers use to get rid of the hoard of job-hunters at their gates. *"We will keep your resume on file, and should anything . . ."* is considered to be kinder than *"Please don't bother us again."*

#2: Success Rate: Only 7%

Answering ads in professional or trade journals, appropriate to your field.

Method: This involves answering ads that appear in journals appropriate to your field. They're similar to the 'help wanted ads' that would be found in newspapers, online or in print.

Success Rate: This results in finding a job for 7 out of every 100 people who use this method.

Reward for Using This Method: Professional journals are comparable to 'niche sites' on the Internet. (Indeed, many journals are online, with their ads.) Employers place ads here when they want to speak to people in their own profession. These ads are targeted at job-hunters 'in the know.' This method works for you if you are experienced in your profession, and if you are willing to relocate, as the ads will rarely turn out to be in your geographical area.

Biggest Problem with This Method: As a job-hunter you're restricted just to advertised vacancies, in what is called 'the open job-market.' But many employers prefer to hire by word of mouth, thus creating the famous 'hidden job-market,' where vacancies are never advertised.

My Comment: For job-hunters, this is one of those 'just in case' methods, included on lists of job-hunting methods merely to cover all the bases. Ads *may* be here that you won't find anywhere else. But most often, employers use journals as a place to copy ads they've already placed elsewhere.

#3: Success Rate: On Up to 10%

Using the Internet to Look for Job-Postings by Employers

Method: Going online and looking for vacancies that employers are willing to advertise online, either on their own site or on job-boards.

Success Rate: Nobody wants to believe this, considering all the hype we hear about the Internet and job-hunting. But nonetheless, the facts are that in good times, this results in finding a job for only up to 10 out of every 100 people who use this method. In bad times, the odds are worse. That's why you can go down to the library and get on one of their computers, or on your computer at home, and day after day search the 3000+ job-sites on the Internet, without turning up *anything*.

Reward for Using This Method: It will turn up vacancies placed by employers, so long as the kind of job you are looking for has a common title (like, *accountant*) rather than a title you really don't know, or a title that varies from one place to the next.

It also will turn up vacancies if the job you're looking for is in a field that is desperate for new hires. In the past this has included technology, health care, education, government, applied mathematics, and engineering.

Biggest Problem with This Method: Loss of self-esteem, if after searching daily for a month or more, and failing to find anything, you conclude that something must be wrong with You. Result: no job, lowered self-confidence, depression.

My Comment: No, no, no! Something is wrong with this approach, not with You. This method has a much lower success rate than people expect, because employers do not post all their vacancies on the Internet; not by any means. Generally, they prefer to fill vacancies in-house, or by word of mouth, and they only post vacancies on the Internet if they're desperate. Trust me on this. To be sure, this approach does work, but only for something like 10% of those who try it. The other 90% go away empty. The hype about the Internet and jobs is due to the fact that the 10% who *are* successful tell wondrous stories that make you think this is how the Internet *always* works. For everyone but You.

Some examples:

One job-seeker, a systems administrator in Taos, New Mexico, who wanted to move to San Francisco posted his resume at 10 p.m. on a Monday night, on a San Francisco online bulletin board (Craigslist.org). By Wednesday morning he had over seventy responses from employers.

Again, a marketing professional developed her resume following guidance she found on the Internet, posted it to two advertised positions she found there, and within seventy-two hours of posting her electronic resume, both firms contacted her, and she is now working for one of them.

It is not just in the media that you will find such stories. I receive letters, such as: "In May I was very unexpectedly laid off from a company I was with for five years. I was given a copy of your book by a ministry in our church that helps people without jobs. I read the book, and it was a great source of encouragement for me. The day I was laid off I committed my job search to the Lord. He blessed us, provided for us, and gave me peace of mind throughout my job-hunt. The Internet was my lifeline in finding the right job. I did 100% of my job search and research via the Internet. I found all my leads online, sent all my resumes via email, and had about a 25% response rate that actually led to a phone interview or a face-to-face interview. It was a software company that laid me off, and I am [now] going to work for a publishing company, a position I found online."

And yet another: "Thanks to the Internet, I found what I believe to be the ideal job in [just] eight weeks—a great job with a great company and great opportunities. . . ."

#4: Success Rate:
Somewhere Between 5 and 24%

Answering local newspaper ads.

Method: Reading newspapers, online or in print, to find 'help wanted ads' that you can apply for, by resume or by phone, then ultimately in person.

Success Rate: This is an odd one. This method leads to a job for a minimum of 5 but a maximum of 24 out of every 100 people who use this method. The fluctuation between 5% and 24% is due to the level of salary that is being sought; if you want a modest salary (to put it kindly) this method will work for 24 out of every 100 job-hunters who use it. Not bad odds! On the other hand, if you want a high salary, it will only work for 5 out of every 100 job-hunters who try it. In other words, employers offering high salaries tend to go elsewhere than newspapers to find their man, or woman. They expect ideal candidates to be more sophisticated about finding vacancies, than simply reading want ads.

Reward for Using This Method: This works well if you're simply trying to find 'a stop-gap job'—work where you don't care what you have to do, as long as it brings in money— enough to tide you over until a better job comes along that is more to your liking.

Biggest Problem with This Method: Newspapers are dying, in one metropolis after another. Employers don't go to them in anything like the numbers they used to. Now employers prefer to put a sign in the window, or go to local Internet sites like **www.craigslist.org**.

My Comment: If you're looking for local work, this is one of the methods that you should try, as long as you are not looking for a high-paying job. Look in newspaper racks found on downtown street corners in many if not most towns and cities; there are often little local or regional papers, that come out weekly or whatever. And, they have ads. Many of these regional papers are produced by **www.jobdig.com**.

When you're out of work, particularly in brutal economic times, leave no stone unturned.

#5: Success Rate: Somewhere Between 5 and 28%

Going to private employment agencies or search firms for help.

Method: You can find these firms in your phone company's Yellow Pages. 'Search firms' work on a fee basis for employers, but some new ones will help job-hunters on occasion. 'Private employment agencies' are businesses, some of them well-known names, that link job-hunters and employers. What they essentially do is phone up employers asking if there are any positions they are trying to fill. If so, the employer gives the agency a 'listing.' These agencies then act as go-betweens, trying to find job-hunters to fill those listings. If the agency you go to, happens to have an employer-listing for someone with your skills, they will send you over for an interview. If you get hired, the agency gets paid a fee. Either by you or by the employer. It all depends. Most often, it's you.

Success Rate: This method results in finding a job for a minimum of 5, and a maximum of 28 out of every 100 people who use this method. The range is for the same reason as noted in #4.

Reward for Using This Method: Finds vacancies that may be unadvertised, but the agency dug them up for you, through their aggressive phoning of employers—or other initiatives.

Biggest Problem with This Method: The fee. The agency is going to charge *someone* a fee; if they charge the employer, no problem (to you, anyway). But if they charge you, it can be a big problem. You must ask, going in: *who pays the fee if I find employment through you? And what is that fee?*

My Comment: The success of this method used to be about as good or as bad as perusing newspaper ads. However, in recent years the success rate has risen in the case of women but not of men: in one study, 27.8% of female job-hunters found a job within two months, by going to private employment agencies. This is in line with the fact that during this brutal economy, women generally have a somewhat lower unemployment rate than men.

Other Job-Hunting Methods in the Least Effective Category

For the sake of comprehensiveness we should note that there are at least three other methods for trying to find jobs, that technically fall into this category of Worst Ways. Those three are:

1. Going to places where employers pick up workers, such as union halls. Overall, this has an 8% success rate. Among those who go to a union hiring hall, however, there is good and bad news. On the one hand, union members who are in the trades have a 22% success rate, using this method, even though it is often for short-term contracts. The bad news: this can't help a lot of people because only 7.9% of non-governmental workers in the U.S. are union members currently.

2. Taking a written civil service exam. This has a 12% success rate, in leading to a job.

3. Going to the state/federal employment service office. This has a 14% success rate in finding work.

Okay, so much for the Worst Ways to hunt for a job—the ones that pay off least, for the time you spend on them. If you have only limited time and energy to give to your job-hunt, you'll probably be wise to give the previous methods only as much time as they deserve. (A 10% success rate means give it only 10% of your total job-hunting time *that week*.)

The Five Best Ways to Hunt for a Job

We turn now to the five best ways to hunt for a job, in my forty years' study of this field. If your job-hunt stretches on for weeks or even months, these are the strategies I recommend you start with, in case your energy runs out before you've finished working your way through all eighteen methods. I will list these five in reverse order. That is to say, I will save the best one for last. We'll start with #5.

#5: A 33% Success Rate

You ask your network for any job leads.

Method: You ask them one simple question: do you know of any jobs at the place where you work—or elsewhere? You ask this of your family. Your friends. Former professors or teachers at any school you ever attended. Business associates. Anyone and everyone you know.

Success Rate: This search method has a 33% success rate. That is, out of every 100 people who use this search method, 33 will get lucky, and find a job thereby. Sixty-seven job-hunters will not—if they use only this method to search for work.

Payoff for Using This Method: If they know of any vacancy in a field that interests you, they can introduce and recommend you. You don't walk in as just a stranger.

Biggest Problem with This Method: The vacancies, if they know of any, may not be in a field that interests you. But you may be tempted to try to make yourself fit the job, rather than making the job fit what it is that you want for your life.

My Comment: You may think a success rate of 33% doesn't deserve to be called one of the five best ways to look for a job. I agree, but it's all relative. "The fifth best" out of the eighteen job-hunting methods that are out there, isn't necessarily saying much. But to put things in perspective, do note that this method's success rate is almost five times higher than the success rate for resumes. In other words, by asking for job leads from your family and friends, you have an almost five times better chance of finding a job, than if you had just sent out your resume.

#4: A 47% Success Rate

Knocking on the door of any employer, factory, or office that interests you, whether they are known to have a vacancy or not.

Method: You go after places that interest you, preferably small employers (100 employees or less) rather than the large behemoths.

Success Rate: This results in finding a job for 47 out of every 100 people who use this method.

Payoff for Using This Method: You often happen upon a vacancy that just got created. One man I know was a draftsman, and he walked into a place that interested him at 11 A.M. The draftsman who was working there had just quit at 10 A.M. The relieved boss hired our man, on the spot.

Then again, using this method you may help to create a new job there, if they meet you, like you, and want to hold on to you—and never let you go.

Biggest Problem with This Method: It is not for the timid or the terminally shy. It takes a bit of moxie to knock on a door, and ask for five minutes of their time, without prior appointment.

My Comment: It is amazing to me how often this job-hunting method works. You fear, ahead of time, that your visit may be intrusive and unwelcome and you will be rudely sent away; and indeed that does happen, but would you really want to work at such a place? 'The right place' is as much a matter of what kind of people work there, as it is a matter of what do they do there. You'll usually do better with small employers (in this case, fifty or less employees).

#3: A 69% Success Rate

By yourself, using the index to your phone book's Yellow Pages to identify subjects or fields of interest to you in the town or city where you want to work.

Method: Once identified, you then look at the listings in the Yellow Pages to identify organizations that look interesting; then you call them up (or go visit them) to ask if they are hiring for the type of position you can do, and do well.

Success Rate: This results in finding a job for 69 out of every 100 people who use this method. Your instinct tells you that it shouldn't work so well; but it does.

Payoff for Using This Method: Even in the worst of times, some employers are still hiring. I saw three "Help Wanted" signs in store windows just last week. But these jobs remain part of the 'hidden job-market,' meaning they are not advertised in the places where you would normally expect them to be. This method often uncovers them.

Biggest Problem with This Method: During brutal economic times job-creation diminishes, so this method doesn't appear to work as well as it does in good times. Also, phoning people doesn't work as well as it did in the pre-"*Please listen carefully to the following menu*" days.

My Comment: Still, it works ten times better than a resume-based job-hunt.

#2: A 70% Success Rate

**Working with others in a job-club,
using the index to your phone book's Yellow Pages
to identify subjects or fields of interest to you in the
town or city where you want to work.**

Method: Same as the previous method, except here you work with a partner to identify leads. Moreover, you share with the rest of the group what kind of job you are looking for.

Success Rate: This results in finding a job for 70 out of every 100 people who use this method.

Payoff for Using This Method: Say you're in a job-club that has 48 other members. With this method, once you tell them what you're looking for, you get an extra 48 pairs of eyes looking on your behalf, and an extra 48 pairs of ears listening on your behalf—all the time that they're out there looking after their own interests.

Biggest Problem with This Method: Nathan Azrin invented this method back in 1973. It had an 84% success rate; but most so-called 'job-clubs' today do not follow his model religiously, so the success rate has declined to 70% or less. Azrin's job-club model was all about action, doing phoning in the morning, going out and doing the actual job-hunt every afternoon; while many so-called job-clubs today are instead about inspiration, pep talks, and encouragement; but the actual job-hunt occurs outside the group.

My Comment: This is a personal comment. I was talking to Nathan just the other day (it is April 2009, as I write) and he would like to know of any job-clubs that are still following his model religiously. You will know who you are. Please let me know you exist, and I will convey the message to Nathan (my email is fivedayworkshop@aol.com).

#1: An 86% Success Rate

**Do homework on yourself, taking inventory
in detail of all you have to offer and
what you are looking for.**

Method: This homework revolves around three simple words: What, Where, How.

1. WHAT. This has to do with your skills, specifically your 'transferable skills.' These are usually **verbs**, like *analyzing, organizing, researching, communicating,* etc. You need to inventory and identify what skills you have *that you most enjoy using.* I didn't say: that are most marketable. No, these are the ones you enjoy using the most. That's usually because you're best at them. They are called

your transferable skills, because they are transferable to any field/career that you choose, regardless of where you first picked them up.

2. WHERE. This has to do with job environments. Think of yourself as a flower. Every flower has an environment where it blossoms. In that sense, you are like a flower. You need to decide where you would most enjoy using your skills, because that is where you will do your most effective work. Experts call these your 'fields of fascination,' or just 'fields.' These are usually **nouns**, like *technology, finance, the arts, chemistry, automobiles, criminal justice, nursing, hospitality,* etc.

3. HOW. This is a matter of how you find out the answers to five things. You want to know how to define:

a) the *manner* in which you perform your job. (These are usually **adjectives** or **adverbs**, such as *thoroughly, quickly, economically, expertly,* etc.) They are often called 'traits.'

b) the *job titles* (it may be several) of work that involves your transferable skills in your fields of fascination.

c) the names of *organizations* (in your preferred geographical area) that have such jobs to offer (we call these organizations your *targets*).

d) the name of that *person* in each target organization who actually has the power to hire you.

e) how can you best *approach* that person to show him or her how your skills and knowledge of that field can help them with their goals and challenges.

Success Rate: To be sure, this doesn't feel like a job-hunting method, but it is. And according to records kept for years, this method has an 86 percent success rate. In other words, 86 out of every 100 people who use this method succeed in not only finding work, but *truly rewarding work* that matches the gifts they have.

Such an effectiveness rate is astronomically higher than virtually every other job-hunting method there is. For example, *doing-homework-on-yourself* works 12 times better than resumes, when you're looking for work. This means, that by doing the hard thinking this method requires, you have a 1,200 percent better chance of finding a job than if you just send out resumes!

To toss in a dose of realism here, it doesn't work for everyone; 14 job-hunters out of 100 will still not find the jobs that are out there, if they use only this method to search for them.

Payoff for Using This Method: Well, there are three, actually:

1. You can more accurately define *to yourself* just exactly what you're looking for, beneath the shifting shape of job-titles. In a brutal economy, job-titles like 'accountant' just aren't detailed enough. New thinking is called for: you are *not* 'an accountant' (or whatever). You are *a person, who* . . . You are a person who has these skills and these experiences.

2. You can more accurately describe *to your family, friends, and networks* just exactly what you're looking for, in detail. Not just *"Uh, I'm out of work; let me know if you hear of anything,"* but exactly what kind of work, in what environment.

3. Lastly, you can more accurately describe *to employers* exactly what is unique about you, and what you bring to the table that, say, nineteen other competitors for this vacancy don't bring, in spite of the fact that their experience and skills look as though they were equal to yours.

Biggest Problem with This Method: It involves work. 'Thinking' kind of work. Most job-hunters therefore avoid it. Takes too much time. Demands too much thinking.

It certainly is not for the lazy, nor for those looking for the easy way out of their unemployment situation. (It actually can be done in a full weekend, or on six successive Monday nights; but why spoil people's fantasy that they won't do it because it would take forever.)

My Comment: You know, I wondered for years why this particular approach to job-hunting worked so well. It was obvious that it did. Careful records were kept by its early practitioners such as John Crystal, Arthur Miller, Bernard Haldane, and Sidney Edlund. No doubt it worked. Superbly. My curiosity was: Why?

I couldn't come up with any satisfactory answer, for a long time. And then I went through the experiences I described at the beginning of this chapter, where I learned that not only must you keep your eyes always on the target you are trying to reach, but that *the more detailed your picture of that target* the more likely you are to reach it.

Case in point:

When you're throwing, not just the clothes hamper, but the corner of the hamper.

When you're driving, not just the lane, but the very center of the lane.

And: when you're looking for meaningful work, not just a job-title, but the details of the work beneath the title: using what transferable skills? in what fields of fascination to you? surrounded by what kinds of people? serving what kinds of customers? meeting and solving what kinds of challenges? furthering what values or ideals? etc.

It was a universal truth: *you must keep your eyes always on the target you are trying to reach. And the more detailed your picture of that target, the more likely you are to reach it.*

It suddenly made perfect sense to me, why this was, and is, the most effective way to look for a job.

Vision is everything.

So, what have we learned from this chapter?

How about this: you're out of work. You're comforted by all the tools at your disposal: the Internet, ads, agencies, resumes, networking. And yet the most effective method of finding meaningful work depends not on the tools you have. It depends instead on *your Vision. Your Vision of Yourself, and what you want to do with your life.*

5

The Internet: The 10% Solution

A RECENT (3/27/09) NIELSEN Company study found that in the U.S. the average adult is spending eight and a half hours a day in front of a screen—be it a computer screen, cell phone screen, TV screen, DVDs, sports channels, video games, or whatever.

So naturally, when we are out of work, our instinct is to move to a screen for help: in this case, our computer screen and the Internet. In the U.S., at least three out of every four adults have access to the Internet.

How much does this help us find work? Statistics change over time, but past studies have shown that this results in a job for 10 out of every 100 job-hunters who try it. The other 90 have to turn elsewhere to locate those vacancies that do exist.

Still, if it works for you, you will thank your lucky stars for the Internet. So, I call this "the 10% Solution." It solves job-hunters' problems in 10% of cases; therefore it deserves 10% of every job-hunter's *time*, just in case. But not more than that. Unless you like beating your head against a brick wall.

Let's rehearse what we as job-hunters can find on the Internet:

The Internet is a place where employers go, to list *some* of their vacancies, but by no means *all*.

The Internet is a place where job-hunters go, to find those vacancies, or to hunt for employers regardless of known vacancies. It is also the place where job-hunters list their own availability, in case some bright-eyed employer is prowling the Internet—and notices.

And for completeness let us add: the Internet is also a place for *advice*, *career counseling*, *testing*, *researching* careers, industries, salaries, companies, or individuals who have the power to hire you, and actually *making contact* with people who may be able to do you some good (*networking*).

In this connection, I should mention that on the Internet there are free guides to the entire job-hunt process. In addition to my own website, jobhuntersbible.com, there are six sites I recommend as most comprehensive and helpful:

www.job-hunt.org run by Susan Joyce.

www.jobstar.org run by Mary Ellen Mort.

www.rileyguide.com run by Margaret F. Dikel.

www.quintcareers.com run by Dr. Randall Hansen.

www.cacareerzone.org run by the California Career Resource Network. Once you are on the home page, it gives you a choice between running the site under Text, Graphic, or Flash. Choose Graphic; I ran Flash, but it had serious hiccups at the time I tried it. Still, this site has nice self-tests, and much else. So, run it under Graphic, if Flash fails.

Now we turn to job-search.

What should I know before I start my job-search on the Internet?

In a word, *your target*. Many job-hunters "network" without any thought to what they're networking for. And when nothing works out, month after month, they express bewilderment.

"But I've been networking, just like everyone says I should!" they cry. I look at them, incredulous. "To what end?" I reply.

They wander like rudderless ships, drifting down the coast, carried briefly into any harbor they encounter, before being carried again out to sea. They have no destination; there is no city they are trying to reach. They're relying on plain blind Luck. "*Maybe I'll stumble across something that sounds interesting.*" Yes, maybe you will. But most likely, you won't.

Having no clear target is the reason so many people are out of work during this brutal economic time.

So, before you go on the Internet define a target, a destination you are trying to reach. Write it down, and keep it at your elbow:

1. What kind of work are you looking for? What job-title specifically? *on or off the Internet.*

2. What industry or field are you looking for? *on or off the Internet.*

3. What section of the country are you looking for? *on or off the Internet.*

4. What kind of salary are you looking for? *on or off the Internet.*

If you can't answer these questions with words, close your eyes and try to visualize what kind of work would give you the greatest delight to do. Sometimes a picture is worth a thousand words. As they say.

Okay, then what sites should I go to, to hunt for whatever vacancies employers have decided to post on the Internet?

1. Omnibus Search Engines. These are sites which search for all the job listings on the Internet, thus saving you from having to go and visit each job-board, one by one.

    Examples: Simplyhired.com. This site claims to have over 5 million job listings, worldwide, as of 3/31/09.

    Indeed.com. This site claims to discover and index over 50 million jobs per year.

2. The Famous Job Boards.
    Examples: careerbuilder.com
    monster.com
    hotjobs.yahoo.com

3. Community Bulletin Boards.
    Example: craigslist.org

4. Niche Sites for Jobs in Specific Fields or Industries. To turn these up, for the industry that interests you, put the name of the industry and the word "jobs" into Google's search engine.

    If you have no idea what industry you are hunting for, but you do know the basic building blocks of the job you are seeking, then put into your favorite search engine, such as Google, your skills, and field of interest (in one or three words) and see what industries these

point to. Be specific. Not just your favorite skills—
"writing researching speaking"—but skills and fields
(for example) "writing renewable energy researching."
That sort of narrowing down.

Example of a niche site: dice.com. This is for tech
or IT jobs.

5. **Social Networking Sites.** Job-hunters are paying a lot of
attention to these particular sites these days, inasmuch
as over five million unemployed people are now 'networking': trying to meet as many people as they possibly can, because—well, that's what they've been told to
do. Networking is 'hot.' That doesn't necessarily mean
it will lead to a job.

These sites, like all the previous ones, may turn up
jobs; but they particularly excel at turning up names
of people. These sites help you look for people in your
favorite industry; they may know of vacancies not being
advertised as yet (thus comprising the so-called "hidden job market").

Anyway, if these sites have jobs, here is where they
can be found:

LinkedIn.com/jobs. LinkedIn claims to be "the"
professional network on the Web; certainly it is the
most talked about. It has over 35 million members, in
170 industries, at this writing. 'Professional' doesn't
mean white collar necessarily. Construction workers,
for example, list themselves on this site; construction
companies know that, and come here searching for
them—when there's work to be had. There are similar
sites to LinkedIn, notably plaxo.com. A complete list
can be found at http://bit.ly/SC4l in Wikipedia.

Twitterjobsearch.com. Twitter has at least 6 million "users" who send "tweets." (Only 140 characters or spaces at a time, as you probably know.) **Twistoridesktop.com** allows you to search Twitter with keywords—or clusters of them—of your own choosing. **Exectweets.com** follows top business leaders; you can search by field or industry. **WeFollow.com** drills down into Twitter, and lets you search categories to see who's "twittering" from that category or industry. And there is also **Twitdir.com**; dir is short for "directory." Incidentally, **TweetDeck.com** is a wonderful way to organize your social contacts on the Internet.

Jobs.MySpace.com. MySpace has over 106 million members worldwide. It currently has the largest U.S. base among all the social networking sites, but that's predicted to change by January 2010, when Facebook will likely surpass it.

Facebook.com. There are over 20 applications you can use within Facebook to find a job; a nice list of them is to be found at **http://blog.bincsearch.com/?p=1108**; Facebook currently has over 42 million U.S. members, over 175 million worldwide.

There! There are the five kinds of sites that you should explore, if you're looking for vacancies advertised on the Internet by employers.

Why doesn't the Internet work better at finding jobs?

It mostly has to do with the fact that job-hunters and employers like to look for each other, in almost exactly opposite ways. Resumes and the Internet are high on a job-hunter's preferred list; not necessarily on an employer's. You can see this from the following diagram:

Many If Not Most Employers Hunt for Job-Hunters in the Exact Opposite Way from How Most Job-Hunters Hunt for Them

The Way a Typical Employer Prefers to Fill a Vacancy

1 **6**

From Within: Promotion of a full-time employee, or promotion of a present part-time employee, or hiring a former consultant for in-house or contract work, or hiring a former "temp" full-time. Employer's thoughts: *"I want to hire someone whose work I have already seen."* (A low-risk strategy for the employer.)

Implication for Job-Hunters: See if you can get hired at an organization you have chosen—as a temp, contract worker, or consultant—aiming at a full-time position only later (or not at all).

2 **5**

Using Proof: Hiring an Unknown Job-Hunter who brings proof of what he or she can do, with regards to the skills needed.

Implication for Job-Hunters: If you are a programmer, bring a program you have done—with its code; if you are a photographer, bring photos; if you are a counselor, bring a case study with you; etc.

3 **4**

Using a Best Friend or Business Colleague: Hiring someone whose work a trusted friend of yours has seen (perhaps they worked for him or her).

Implications for Job-Hunters: Find someone who knows the person-who-has-the-power-to-hire at your target organization, who also knows your work and will introduce you two.

4 **3**

Using an Agency They Trust: This may be a recruiter or search firm the employer has hired; or a private employment agency—both of which have checked you out, on behalf of the employer.

5 **2**

Using an Ad They Have Placed (online or in newspapers, etc.).

6 **1**

Using a Resume: Even if the resume was unsolicited (if the employer is desperate).

The Way a Typical Job-Hunter Prefers to Fill a Vacancy

Besides this ironic fact illustrated by the above diagram, there is another.

When an employer comes on the Internet looking for someone to hire, they are essentially engaging in an activity called 'job-matching.'

Now, job-matching works by using job-titles.

And job-titles are, generally speaking, a big problem for the Internet. Not a big problem when you're looking for a job that has a simple title, such as "secretary," or "gardener," or "nurse," or "driver," or "waitress," or "mechanic," or "salesperson." Any of these should turn up a lot of matches.

But, you may be looking for a job that various employers call by differing titles, and that's an entirely different ballgame. If you guess wrongly about what they call the job you're looking for, then you and those employers will be like two ships passing in the night, on the Internet high seas. Your faithful, hardworking computer will report back to you in the morning: "No matches," when in fact there actually are. You just didn't guess correctly what title those employers are using. Oops!

Finally, job-titles are a problem for Internet searches because a typical job-board on the Internet may limit you to a prepared list of only two dozen job-titles, from which you must choose. This leaves out the other 20,000 job-titles that are out there in the work world—including, of course, the one that you are searching for, in particular.

So sure, Internet job-matching works. Sometimes. Beautifully. But know ahead of time that you can't count on it necessarily working for You. In the end, it's a big fat gamble that works about 10% of the time. It's a 10% solution to your problem.

6

Do I Need a Resume?

You PROBABLY ALREADY HAVE ONE, whether you want one or not.

Let me explain.

Before the Internet: The 'Old' Resume

No, 'Old' doesn't mean an outdated draft of your resume. 'Old' here means "the kind of resume you've always heard about, since you were a kid."

In the days before the Internet's popularity the only way an employer could learn much about you prior to hiring you, was from a piece of paper that you handed them or mailed to them, ahead of time. On that paper was a summary of what you had done, and where you had been.

It was of course what we call "a resume." It was (and is) also called your curriculum vitae, or C.V. for short. From that piece, or pieces, of paper, the employer was supposed to guess what kind of person you are and what kind of employee you'd be.

And that was about the limit to what an employer could learn about you, save for references or hiring a private detective.

Because the employer's information about you was limited to the paper you handed them, you were in command of what the employer knew; you could omit anything that was embarrassing, or anything from your past that you have long since regretted. You had control over how you came across to a prospective employer.

In the Twenty-First Century: The New Resume

Now, welcome to the twenty-first century. That control is gone. There is a new Resume in town, and if you've been at all active on the Internet—if you've been on Facebook, MySpace, YouTube, or if you have you own website or webcasts or photo album or blog or tweets—then there's hardly any limit to what employers can learn about you. They have only to 'Google' your name and see what turns up. And there you are revealed (or will be) in all your hidden glory.

What will they see? Those impressive achievements you've made, where you far exceeded people's expectations—they're there; but so are those playful photos you've allowed your friends to post on your page, that make you look like an idiot. They're there, too. And more.

All these things, together, comprise your New Resume, a richer body of data about You than your old Resume ever hoped to be. And from this, now, prospective employers can better guess what kind of person you are and what kind of employee you'd be.

Or at least they will think they can, even if personally you feel the Internet is only offering a distorted, 'fun house mirror' picture of you.

So, the answer to the question "will employers need a resume from you," is: actually, they've already got one—if you've been at all active on the Internet. It's The New Resume—*all there is about you on the Internet*—courtesy of Google. And at least half of all employers, at this writing, go looking for this New Resume before they hire you, or anyone else. That number will only increase as time moves on.

So, what can I do about this New Resume, when heaven knows what they'll find?

Actually, you're not as helpless or as vulnerable here, as you might at first suppose. There are actions you can take, and four things you can do—*edit*, *add*, *fill in*, and *expand*—to improve the way you look on the Internet. Let's drill down.

Edit. First of all, think of how you want to come across, when you go in for a job interview. Make a list of adjectives you'd like the employer to think of, when they see you. For example, would you want them to think of you as: *professional? well informed? creative? hard working? team-member? born leader? disciplined? honest? trustworthy? kind?* Or what?

Secondly, 'Google' yourself, and go over everything the search engine pulls up about you. Go over any pages you have put up on social sites like Facebook, or MySpace, or YouTube, or Flickr and look for anything you posted there, or allowed others to post, that would cause a would-be employer to think, "Uh, let's not call them in, after all." Look particularly for unflattering pictures or four-letter text.

If you find anything you don't want an employer to see, you have two options. One is: look to see if the site allows you to choose privacy settings. If it does, choose "friends only" or some narrow permission like that.

Your other option is to remove just the offending item. If you don't know how to remove an item from a particular site, put the following into a search engine like Google: "how to remove an item from my page on Facebook" or whatever. You're hardly the first one with this need to edit. With any site you can name, someone's already figured out how to remove stuff, if it's humanly possible. Trust me. The inventiveness at work out there is mind-boggling.

Add. Next, write and post the Old kind of resume right on top of the New, as it were. Once you've written it, post it everywhere online: on the omnibus job boards, famous job boards, community bulletin boards, and niche sites. Post it, above all, on the actual website of companies that interest you, if their site allows that. (You *have* chosen companies or organizations that interest you, I hope.)

Just remember that this resume—this piece of electronic paper—may be and most probably will be copied to multiple sites, with or without your help. After that, there is really no way for you to ever take it down. It may hang out in cyberspace for the next one hundred years. So, make sure you're pleased with it, before posting.

If you need help, 'Google' "how to write a resume" and you should find oodles of help (a resume's structure is even outlined on Wikipedia).

If after all this advice, you still can't write one to save your life, look up 'resume writers' in the phone book's Yellow Pages. Or ask around, among your friends, for who they think is good. You're interested in not how their resumes *look*, but how many have gotten their clients *an invitation* to come in for a job interview.

During these brutal economic times, this posting of your traditional resume will work better with smaller companies than with large. ("Smaller companies" are typically defined either as those that have 100 employees or less, or those that have 50 employees or less. Probably we need a new vocabulary, like: "small companies" and "small-small companies.")

Don't expect any acknowledgement or reply from companies. Studies have shown that less than 45% of employers ever acknowledge resumes even when posted right on their own site. So, just post the thing, cross your fingers, and pray it has arrived at the right place at the right time.

Why should I post this Old type of resume, when my New Resume is already spread all over the Internet?

Well, let's consider the historic purpose of the Old type of resume.

It has traditionally had but one purpose: to get yourself invited in, for an interview. Nothing more. We have been told that the resume is not there to 'sell you,' or to secure a job. It's only there to get an interview. 'Selling' is what you do after you're in the interview room. It's your task, not the resume's.

So, the traditional advice has been: before you post it read over every single sentence and ask yourself this one question: "Will this make them want to invite me in, for an interview?" If not, omit that sentence. Above all, your resume is no place for 'true confessions.' ("*I kind of botched up, at the end, in that job; that's why they let me go, as I'm sure they'll tell you when you check my references.*") Save that also for the interview room, and near the end of the interview, at that.

But with the advent of the New Resume—*all there is about you, scattered all over the Internet*—a new purpose has been found for your carefully written resume: to summarize in one succinct place what you most want a prospective employer to first see about you. Before they see all the rest.

That done, your next task is to fill in.

Fill In. Next, on any Internet site that allows you to fill out a profile, do it. Fill it out completely. Cross every t, and dot every i. Leave no part of the profile blank unless you have a very good reason. As my friend Guy Kawasaki says, "You should fill out your profile like it's an executive bio, so include past companies, education, affiliations, and activities." Moreover, as time goes on, be sure to keep it up-to-date. There is nothing that makes you look less like a professional than having an obviously outdated profile from two years back or more.

Oh, and get on LinkedIn, if you're not already; it's the site of first resort when someone is curious about you. To help them find you, put a link back to your LinkedIn profile, as part of your email signature.

Expand. Expand your presence on the Internet, so there is a greater likelihood that an employer will trip over you. How to do this? Several ways.

Forums. Professional sites like LinkedIn have forums, or groups, organized by subject matter. So do other social networking sites. Look through the directory of those groups or forums, choose one or two that are related to your industry or interests, and after signing up, speak up regularly whenever you have something to say that will quietly demonstrate you are an expert in this subject area. That way you will get noticed by employers when they're searching for expert talent in these fields.

Blogs. Start a blog (*short for "web log," as you probably know*), if you don't already have one. It doesn't matter what your expertise, if it's related to the job you are looking for, do a blog, and update it regularly.

If you already have a blog, but it roams all over the land, in terms of subject matter, then start a new blog that is more narrowly preoccupied with your area of expertise.

Post helpful articles there, focused on action. Generally speaking, employers are looking for concrete action, rather than lofty philosophical thought. Unless, of course, they represent a think tank.

Let's say you are an expert plumber; you can post entries on your blog that deal with such problems as "how to fix a leaky toilet," etc. That type of thing.

And if you don't know how to blog, there are helpful sites such as **www.blogger.com/start** which can give you detailed instructions.

Videos. If you've been asleep for the past few years, you may not have noticed that presentation is moving more and more to the visual. Otherwise, you're bound to have noticed.

There are the incredibly popular video sites: YouTube is in a class by itself, but there are also Vimeo, Jumpcut, and others.

Then there are the photo sites: Flickr, Picnik, and the like.

And finally let's not forget Netflix and Hulu.

So, if you're trying to expand your presence on the Internet, one of the things you might consider doing is posting a video on your blog. Vimeo and Jumpcut are among the sites which make that easy.

You can add a small video clip even if all you or a friend have is a simple little camera such as the Flip video camcorder, which you can pick up on Amazon for about sixty bucks (used).

Thus our plumber, above, wouldn't have to just write out instructions for fixing a leaky toilet. He could actually demonstrate the steps. A video will make your presence on the Internet more noticeable. Post one, whatever else you do, on YouTube.

In sum, people, including employers, will usually pay more attention to a blog that has video than they will to one that just has text, text, text. In video lurks astonishment, wonder, and joy. Think Paul Potts. Think Susan Boyle.

Web Site. If you're truly determined to expand your presence on the Internet as much as possible, start a website of your own. On your favorite subject or expertise related to the kind of work you're looking for. Go to sites like Yola.com for free help and instructions.

It seems to me that all of these maneuvers are assuming that employers are prowling the Internet looking for job-hunters who could fill their vacancies. But in fact, aren't far fewer employers doing this, during this brutal economy?

Undeniably. But they have friends. Who have friends. These friends may be on the Internet for other reasons than looking for job candidates. But they can't help noticing if someone really stands out, as they're circulating through cyberspace; and they may mention it to an employer friend who could use you, sooner or later.

Also, what you are doing here is assembling a portfolio of resources concerning your talent and achievements, that you can refer prospective employers to, whenever you make contact with them. Thus you will stand out from 19 other candidates whose background superficially looks equal to yours. All of this is hard work, and many if not most job-hunters won't be willing to work this hard at their job-hunt. You will definitely make an impression.

Will you get hired through the Internet? As we saw in the previous chapter, your chances are 10% or less—without all the work in this chapter. With this much work, your chances definitely improve. Though it's hard to put a figure on it.

But it's worth giving it a shot. Just don't pin all your hopes on it. Nor think something's wrong with you, if nothing comes of it. There are other job-hunting strategies, as we have seen.

Conclusion: If you do all the things I suggest in this chapter, and no bright-eyed employer comes to discover you, there are things you can still do. If the Internet won't save you. If resumes won't save you. Then you must save yourself (with God's help).

You've got some hard work ahead. Thinking. You must take the initiative, now, by doing homework on yourself.

7

Looking for The Job You Used to Have

I lost my job, but I liked the kind of work I was doing. How can I find That Kind of job, again?

You begin, of course, with the Internet. Your best friend here is a search engine, such as Google (**www.google.com**). You put several terms into the search engine at the same time: name of the job-title you previously held, your geographical preference, your field, and the word "jobs." See if that turns up anything.

Next, you put the same terms into an omnibus job-search engine such as **Indeed.com** or **SimplyHired.com** that sweeps through many if not most of the Internet's job listings, in one fell swoop.

What do I do if nothing turns up, there?

Well, that wouldn't be surprising. This is a brutal economy, right now, as you know. So, plan B, you've got to do some thinking. Dust off your brain, and ask yourself what jobs would be *related* to what you used to do. Think about questions like these, to find Related Jobs:

1. What supplies, equipment, or support services did you use at your last job? Would the suppliers or manufacturers of that equipment or those materials be willing to tell you other places where their equipment or supplies are used? *For example, if you worked at a digital photo place, would those who supplied the photo paper or the digital equipment be willing to tell you where else their customers are? It can't hurt to ask them. Maybe that information is confidential, but then again, maybe it isn't.* If you do get the names of other places that use the equipment or supplies you are familiar with, don't think they're unapproachable until they have a known vacancy. Once you have their names, you can approach them anyway, and please do. (Somebody there may have quit just that morning.)

2. What machinery or technologies did you learn, master, or improve upon, at your last job? Can you find out what other places use such machinery or technology? Try. You could then approach them and ask them if any of them would be interested in hiring you. Sure, they've cut their staffing due to budget constraints; but they may have cut too close to the bone, and now find they need to hire someone with your skills and experience.

3. Who supplied training or development to you, at your last job? If it was an outside training organization, would they be interested in hiring you—assuming you're good at communication? It doesn't hurt to approach them and ask. Some training places will be losing customers, as their former clients cut back; some training places may be struggling for their own life. But not all. It never hurts to ask.

4. What companies, organizations, or customers did you serve, in your last job? Since they know you, you can approach them and inquire if any of them are in a position to hire someone with your talents and experience.

5. What community or service organizations were interested in, or a participant in, or helped fund any projects you headed up, at your last job? Would any of them be interested in hiring someone with your known talent and experience? Contact them, and ask.

6. What were the skills and problem-solving abilities that you learned or demonstrated at your last job? Can you think of any place that is wrestling with similar problems that would call for those kinds of skills? If so, approach them and ask if they could use you. Remember, in the jargon of management, you are presenting yourself to them as a resource-broker, not a job-beggar.

7. What temp agencies, outsourcing agencies, or subcontractors were used at your last job? Would any of them be interested in hiring you—temporarily, or for a one-time contract, or longer term? Anyway, approach them, and ask.

8. You know your own community, I presume. You sleep, shop, and play there, even if you didn't work there. What kinds of needs does it have, that aren't being taken care of? What kind of services are people willing to pay for, even in brutal times, because they can't—or don't have time to—do them for themselves? Are your skills and experiences such, that you could start your own little business, to fill those needs?

And if I pursue some of these Related Jobs, but come up empty, what should I think about, next?

Take a hard look at your hobbies that you've done in your leisure time, over the years. The late John Crystal used to define leisure as "what you do when no one is telling you what to do." So, what *do* you do when no one is telling you what to do?

Maybe you've spent quite a bit of time on one thing or another, and become something of an informal expert.

Hobbies? What kind of hobbies?

Right off the top of my head, I can think of such hobbies as: antiques, bicycling, birding, boating, camping, cars, collecting, computers, cooking, dance, electronics, exercising, flowers, gardening, horses, hunting, martial arts, math, models, motorcycles, oceanography, pets, photography, scrapbooking, skiing, sewing, and woodworking. More complete lists can be found on the Internet at such sites as http://tinyurl.com/ce86y6 (the site has the memorable name of Buzzle.com).

The question, of course, is: are there any kinds of jobs you could look for, that are related to your favorite hobby? To find out, put your hobby words along with the word "jobs" into your favorite Internet search engine such as Google.

Alternative sources of information: Go to libraries or stores with large magazine sections. Browse. See if there's a magazine that covers your favorite hobby; buy it, and read it from cover to cover to see what kinds of jobs are advertised there.

I see the merit of doing a lot of hard thinking here, but why didn't my old job-title pop up some vacancies during my Internet job-search?

Well, it probably did if you were looking for simple job titles like "accountant" or "plumber" or "secretary."

But with any title more complex, you may indeed turn up nothing. That's because the job-market in general, and various jobs in particular, are always going through a process of shapeshifting.

Shapeshifting, as you may recall, is a common theme in mythology, folklore, and fiction, down through history, in many cultures of the world. The word refers to mythical creatures—shapeshifters—that have the ability to change their shape, size, and physical appearance at will, often as they are moving about, or being pursued. (An apt metaphor therefore for the jobs we may be chasing during our job-hunt.)

This idea of shapeshifting originated of course in biology and human development. If someone were from Mars I could show them several pictures: one of a baby, one of a young child, one of an adolescent, then a forty-year-old, and an eighty-year-old. And they might not guess that this is all the same person, me, in different time periods.

I change shape, and so do you, just not as magically or quickly as in mythology and fiction. But in the end, we are all shapeshifters.

And so are jobs. And, therefore, job-titles.

To see this shapeshifting in the case of one such title, *teacher*, go to http://tinyurl.com/27ofza to view an eight-minute video on YouTube, called "Pay Attention." Click on it, and play it. See how much the work of a *teacher* is shifting shape before our eyes. Eventually the job-title will change as well.

That's what job-titles do. "Personnel director" has become "human resources professional," "librarian" has become "information-management specialist," "salesman" has become "sales manager," and so it goes—on and on and on.

Job-titles are changing all the time, because the job beneath that title has shifted its shape. That's why pursuing your old job-title during your job-hunt often turns up nothing. That old title has now fallen into disuse. At least at some companies or organizations. And you may not have guessed, as yet, what their new title is.

How then do I dig beneath the job-title I used to hold?

You can dig beneath the job-title by learning to analyze jobs in terms of their component parts, even as you can describe a flower in terms of its individual petals.

A job—any job—has seven parts to it. If it were a flower it would have seven petals. The two most important parts to a job are:

1. Your functional/transferable skills.

2. The field you use those skills in.

   The remaining parts of any job are:

3. The working environment, or working conditions, at that job.

4. The people you are working with, or serving, at that job.

5. What your goals are, as you do that work.

6. Geography: what part of the country, or the world, that job has you working in.

7. And finally, what the salary or other compensation is, at that job.

There you have it: beneath an unknown job-title lies *skills, field, work-environment, people, goals, geography,* and *compensation.*

It will do you lots of good if you practice thinking of a job in these terms, rather than in terms of job-title.

What kind of practice?

Well, to keep it simple and familiar, let's try analyzing that job you loved, which you just lost. Or lost a while back.

Even if there was no love lost, try analyzing your last full-time or part-time job, anyway.

To help you here is a little diagram—a Flower diagram, naturally—which you should copy onto a larger piece of blank paper.

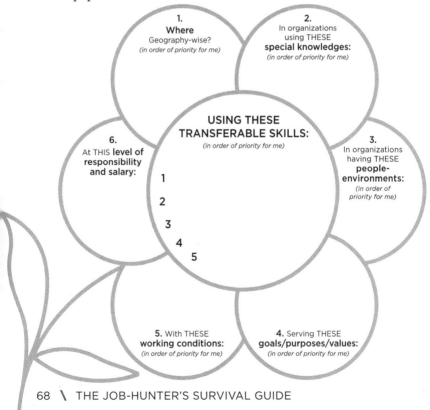

Some guidance in filling it out might be helpful, so here it is:

1. **The Transferable Skills You Used at Your Last Job.** What were the main skills, or your personal favorites, that you used to accomplish the work you did there? Transferable skills can be used in any job or career, because they are not rooted in just one career. Choose three to five from the list below:

Acting	Adapting	Administering	Advising
Analyzing	Arbitrating	Arranging	Assembling
Assessing	Auditing	Budgeting	Building
Calculating	Classifying	Coaching	Collecting
Communicating	Compiling	Composing	Computing
Conceptualizing	Conducting	Conserving	Constructing
Coordinating	Counseling	Creating	Deciding
Defining	Delivering	Designing	Detailing
Detecting	Developing	Devising	Diagnosing
Digging	Directing	Discovering	Dissecting
Distributing	Dramatizing	Drawing	Driving
Editing	Empathizing	Enforcing	Establishing
Estimating	Evaluating	Examining	Expanding
Experimenting	Explaining	Extracting	Filing
Fixing	Formulating	Founding	Gathering
Generating	Guiding	Handling	Helping
Hypothesizing	Identifying	Illustrating	Imagining

Improving	Improvising	Influencing	Informing
Initiating	Innovating	Inspecting	Inspiring
Installing	Instructing	Integrating	Interpreting
Interviewing	Intuiting	Inventing	Inventorying
Investigating	Judging	Leading	Lecturing
Lifting	Listening	Maintaining	Making
Managing	Manipulating	Mediating	Meditating
Memorizing	Mentoring	Modeling	Monitoring
Motivating	Navigating	Negotiating	Observing
Operating	Ordering	Organizing	Originating
Overseeing	Painting	Performing	Persuading
Photographing	Piloting	Planning	Predicting
Preparing	Prescribing	Presenting	Printing
Problem solving	Producing	Programming	Promoting
Proofreading	Protecting	Providing	Publicizing
Purchasing	Questioning	Raising	Reasoning
Recommending	Reconciling	Recording	Recruiting
Reducing	Referring	Rehabilitating	Relating
Remembering	Repairing	Reporting	Representing
Researching	Resolving	Restoring	Retrieving
Scheduling	Selecting	Selling	Sensing
Separating	Serving	Setting up	Sewing
Shaping	Showing	Singing	Sketching
Solving	Sorting	Speaking	Studying
Summarizing	Supervising	Supplying	Symbolizing

Synergizing	Synthesizing	Systematizing	Taking orders
Taking	Teaching	Team-building	Tending
Testing	Training	Transcribing	Translating
Traveling	Treating	Trouble-shooting	Tutoring
Typing	Understudying	Unifying	Uniting
Upgrading	Utilizing	Washing	Writing

Once you have your three to five, put them in order of importance, at that job, then copy them to the center circle of the Flower diagram (Transferable Skills).

2. **The Special Knowledges or Field at Your Last Job.** What field was your last job in? What special knowledges did your job expect you to be familiar with? List no more than three to five. Here is a sampler to get you going:

Aerospace	Agriculture	Airlines	Architecture
Arts	Automobiles	Banking	Biotechnology
Business	Chemistry	Communications	Computers
Construction	Consulting	"Disabilities"	Education
Elder care	Electronics	Energy	Engineering
Environment	Exports	Farming	Finances
Fitness	Food services	Forestry	Fund-raising
Government	Green technologies	Health care	Human resources
Insurance	IT	Journalism	Law
Library sciences	Manufacturing	Media	Medicine

Mining	Military	Mortuary science	Nonprofit
Office equipment	Oil/gas	Organics	Pharmaceutics
Programming	Public affairs	Publishing	Real estate
Recruiting	Recycling	Research	Restaurants
Retail	Social services	Sports	Training
Transportation	Web services	Wind farming	Other
Antiques	*Colors*	*Fashion*	*Flowers*
Graphics	*Languages*	*Music*	*Other*

Put your choice(s) on petal #2, in the Flower diagram (Special Knowledges).

3. **The People You Served, or Served With, at Your Last Job.** List the characteristics of the people you loved working with, or serving, there. Here is a sampler of characteristics you might find were important to you, at that job. Choose any number of them, up to ten.

Accurate	Achievement oriented	Adaptable	Adept at having fun
Adventuresome	Appreciative	Astute	Attentive
Calm	Cautious	Charismatic	Competent
Consistent	Cooperative	Courageous	Creative
Decisive	Deliberate	Dependable	Diligent
Diplomatic	Discreet	Dynamic	Empathetic
Energetic	Enthusiastic	Experienced	Firm
Flexible	Impulsive	Independent	Innovative

Knowledgeable	Loyal	Lots of energy	Methodical
Open-minded	Outgoing	Patient	Perceptive
Persevering	Practical	Professional	Protective
Punctual	Reliable	Resourceful	Responsible
Self-motivated	Sensitive	Sophisticated	Supportive
Sympathetic	Tactful	Thorough	Versatile

Put your choices in their order of importance to you, on petal #3 in the Flower diagram (People Environments).

4. **The Goals Your Work Was Trying to Achieve, at Your Last Job.** It's easy to keep busy, at a job. But that busyness is meaningless unless it's working toward some end. So, when you were busy there, what were you trying to achieve?

I will list some broad goals here. Pick or choose the one that seems to you was the overall, if unspoken, goal there. If you don't see anything that applies, then invent your own definition of what you were trying to achieve at that job. If "just keeping busy" is your answer, then think of what goal you would *like* to have been working toward:

Goal #1. You were working with the human Mind; you were trying to bring more knowledge, truth, or clarity into the world. (If so, how? and concerning what?)

Goal #2. You were working on the human Body; you were trying to deal with the human need for shelter, food, and clothing; you were trying to bring more wholeness, fitness, or health into the world, more binding up of the body's wounds and strength, more feeding of the hungry, and clothing of the poor. (If so, what was the particular issue your work was focused on, there?)

Goal #3. You were working with the Eyes or other senses; you were trying to bring more beauty into the world. (If so, what kind of beauty: art, music, flowers, photography, painting, staging, decorating, crafts, clothing, jewelry, or what? in that job.)

Goal #4. You were working with the human Heart; you were trying to bring more love and compassion into the world, in your work there. (If so, love or compassion for whom? Or for what?)

Goal #5. You were working with the human Will, or conscience; you were trying to bring more morality, more justice, more righteousness, more honesty into the world. (If so, in what areas of human life or history, in particular? And in what geographical area?)

Goal #6. You were working with the human Spirit; you were trying to bring more laughter, more spirituality, more faith, more compassion, more forgiveness, more love for God, into the world. (If so, with what ages, people, or with what parts of human life?)

Goal #7. You were working on the Earth; you were trying to ensure there is more protection of this fragile planet, more exploration—not exploitation—of this island in the Universe. (If so, which problems or challenges in particular, were you trying to deal with, in that job?)

Enroll your target goal at your last job, in your own words, on petal #4 in the Flower diagram. Next?

5. **The Working Conditions at Your Last Job.** To begin with, were you working indoors, or out? Were you pretty constant as to place, or did you travel a lot? Were you free to keep your own hours, or did you have to punch in on a time clock? Were you pretty much working alone, or were you a constant member of a team? Were you given lots of room for your creativity or was your job pretty much prescribed as to what you did? Were you overly supervised, until you could just scream, or were you undersupervised, so you had to guess a lot as to what you were supposed to do next? Those are the kinds of questions that the subject "working conditions" refers to. Put the chief characteristics that stand out in your mind about your last job, and then enroll them on petal #5 on the Flower diagram (Working Conditions).

6. **The Salary or Compensation You Had at Your Last Job.** This petal #6 (Responsibility and Salary) should be easy to fill out. You know what you were paid, you know at what level you operated within the company or organization.

And lastly,

7. **Where, Geographically, Your Last Job Was Located.** Chances are, it's where you still live; but maybe not. Put down where the job was located, here on the petal at the eleven o'clock position on the Flower diagram (it's labeled #1, because the central part of the Flower diagram has no number). If you want to go the extra

mile, if you liked the location, put down three reasons why you liked it.

That's it?

Yes, that's it. You've dug beneath the job-title to what it is you essentially did, in your last job (never mind what title they gave it). But now that you know how to do the analyzing, we turn in the next chapter to your filling out the same diagram—only this time with respect to your future career, your dream job.

This involves your taking inventory of yourself. Yes, I know, I know: this seems so silly. You've lived with yourself all these years, and you certainly should know by now who you are.

Trouble is: it's not just jobs that have shifted shape. You have shapeshifted, too. I hope. As John Cardinal Newman said: "To grow is to change, and to become perfect is to change often." So a new inventory of you is essential during this brutal economic time.

Conclusion: Here is the ultimate truth if you want to live a life that matters: *You shouldn't decide what work to do, until you first know just who you presently are.*

For, what you do should flow directly from who you *are*. That is the key to living a life that makes a difference.

8

Looking for Your Dream Job

"For everything there is a season, and a time for every purpose under heaven: a time to be born, and a time to die; a time to plant, and a time to pluck up that which is planted; . . . a time to break down, and a time to build up. . . . He hath made everything beautiful in its time." (Ecclesiastes 3:1ff)

It is the phrase "a time to break down and a time to build up" that catches our attention, here.

In the previous chapter, we saw how to *break down* a job into its component parts. Here, we are going to do just the opposite: *build up* component parts into a job. *Breaking down* is the key to understanding a job we once had. *Building up* is key to understanding a job we would like to have. At its best, *a dream job.*

This phrase "dream job" is widely misunderstood. It is commonly understood as a 'cushy' job: one with a large income, little responsibility, and loads of freedom to choose what you do, day by day. *What a dream job!*

In real life, a dream job is not that, at all. It is not like a suit off the rack, one dream job fits all; rather, it is like a suit custom-tailored to fit you, and only you. Your dream job is work that flows from, and has an essential connection to, who you are. It is a marriage of *doing* and *being*. It is work that fits *you* like a glove.

Is such-and-such a dream job? Well, everything depends on who you are, what stuff you're made of, and what gifts and passions excite you. A dream job is work tailored to fit *that*.

So, to find *your* dream job requires an up-to-date inventory of your current shapeshifting human self. Incidentally, you may recall that "research on yourself" is the most effective method of job-hunting: it has an 86% success rate, which is twelve times the success rate of resumes. (Go back, and re-read pages 40–44, now.)

Okay, so I should start (or restart) my job-hunt now, by doing research, or homework, on myself. How do I go about doing that?

There are four ways you can go. I will start with the least effective, and go to the most effective.

1. You can write a thorough resume of your life and experience so far. This is a resume for your eyes only, for now. It's for self-examination, not for getting an employer's invitation to come in and see them.

     The problem with this approach: *your resume is a history of your past, with all its constraints, and therefore puts a straitjacket on your visions of the future. It tends to be preoccupied with what makes you 'marketable,' not what makes you fulfilled. You can end up feeling like a square peg jammed into a round hole.*

2. **You can sit down and on one piece of paper (not more) write down everything you can think of, about yourself.** The color of your eyes. That summer at camp when you were six. The dreams you had when you were twenty. Write small. Get it all on one sheet. Then put a graphic of some kind (a stick figure?) on that paper, and when you are done writing (it could take several days as your memory slowly kicks in with new recall every eight hours), go back, take a gander at the whole sheet, and after some thought, circle the ten most important things about you, on that paper. That done, consider what those ten most important things about you have to suggest about the kind of dream job you would most love to find. This is of course your opinion only. And it is for your eyes only.

The problem with this approach: *you are a human being, which means that in one way or another you belong to a community. This approach makes no use of that community; you toil, and write, and analyze, all by yourself. Your brain may let you down, and turn into a mental ice-cube.*

3. **Go take an online "test."** Go take an online "test." The most popular are those based on the "RIASEC" system. They can be found at **CareerPlanner.com**, **CareerKey .org**, **self-directed-search.com**, and O*Net. You can also try the Career Interests Game at **http://tinyurl .com/7wdsh**. All of them are a quick sounding of who you are, in terms of categories originally defined by the late John Holland. There is usually a charge, in the end, for each "test" except in the case of O*Net.

The problem with this approach: *these "tests" try to make you fit into categories that have a three-letter Holland 'code.' You probably won't like the jobs it ends up recommending for you. One thing you might try: take your 'code', let's say it's SIA, and rearrange it into its six alternative forms: SIA, SAI, ASI, AIS, ISA, IAS. Look up the jobs recommended with each.*

4. Last, and most effective, by far: by yourself, or better yet, with the help of two other friends, do 'the Flower exercise' which we saw in the previous chapter. Except that here you are not trying to break down a previous job into its component parts. You are here trying to build up a vision of your dream job out of its component parts. You are here analyzing not "what was," but "what you would like to be" in the times ahead. I'll tell you how to fill it out, in a minute. But let us observe here the great virtue of this approach: it doesn't start with the job-market in mind. It starts with You, in all your great detail.

The problem with this approach: *only one thing— the time and dedication it requires. True, there are millions of job-hunters who are putting in a lot of time on their job-search. They live on their computer, they haunt all the familiar places, they go sleepless, their patience has long since worn thin. They're obviously willing to put in the time on their job-search which this method requires. They've just got to change what they're doing with their time.*

On the other hand, sad to relate, many unemployed college grads now living at home have recently been found devoting just one hour a week to their job-search. To them this method surely looks like work. Correct that. This is work. It certainly takes more than one hour a week.

Okay, I get it. How do I go about this thorough self-inventory, using the Flower exercise?

Copy, again, on a large piece of paper, the Flower diagram that you will see below. Then start filling it in, according to the directions in the right-hand column of the chart you will find on the following page. Fill in every petal except the central petal. When you're done with all the others, read the special instructions for "Transferable Skills," on the pages following the chart, as you finally turn to filling in the central petal.

My Dream Job

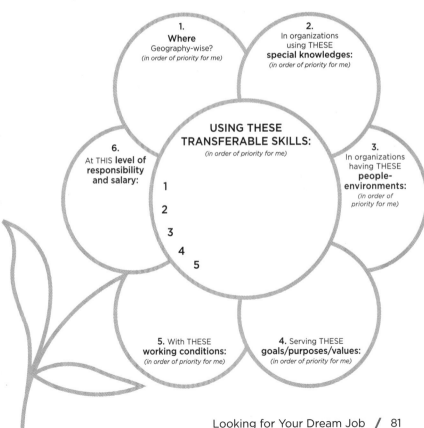

	Job You Used to Have	Your Dream Job
	Broken down, using exercises in the previous chapter (7)	Built from the ground up, using exercises later in this chapter (8)
	You've already done this (if not, go do it now, please, please).	This is what you're going to do in this chapter.
Components	This was for practice.	This is for real.
Job-Title	*A single title, known when you begin*	**Probably multiple titles, unknown 'til the end**
Breaking Down (Job into Components) or Building Up (Components into Job)	⬇	⬆
Transferable Skills	*Taken from what that job required, using the table on pages 69–71.*	Your favorite Transferable Skills that you would like to use in a future job (taken from the grid, pages 85–88, and the seven little blogs from your past).
Field or Special Knowledges	*Taken from what that job required, using the table on pages 71–72.*	Your favorite Fields or Knowledges you would like to use your skills with, in a future job *(taken from the table on pages 71–72, or elsewhere).*
The People You Serve, or Serve With	*Taken from what that job required, using the table on pages 72–73.*	Your favorite kinds of People you would like to serve, or serve with, in the future *(taken from the table on pages 72–73, or elsewhere).*
Your Goal or What You Want to Achieve	*Taken from what that job required, using the list on pages 73–74.*	What Goal you would most like to achieve, long-range or short, in the work you do in the future *(using the list on pages 73–74, or elsewhere).*
Working Conditions	*Taken from what that job required, with paragraph 5 on page 75 as guidance.*	What are the Working Conditions under which you could do your most effective work, in the future *(with paragraph 5 on page 75 as guidance).*
Salary or Compensation	*Taken from what that job paid.*	The level at which you would like to work: boss? team member? consultant? Salary: minimum? max?
Geography	*Taken from where that job was located.*	Three *factors* that describe where you would like your dream job to be located, (e.g., "snow" country, near beach, in a large city? etc.)

Commentary about filling out the Transferable Skills Petal in the Flower diagram: In the previous chapter, you used a list to identify the skills that you used in your last job, whether you wanted to use those particular skills, or not. The job demanded them. End of story.

Here, you are starting at the other end of the tunnel: what skills would you *like* to be able to use in a future job? (We'll go looking for *what* kind of job that would be, later.) The best way to do this is to write a story (or short *blog*). A story of something you did where you really enjoyed yourself. This story, and all the other six you will eventually write, one by one, should exhibit the structure: *goal, obstacle, how you overcame it step by step, result, how much you made, saved, or whatever*. Write it out, in some detail. Call this one "Story #1."

When you are done writing, turn to the Transferable Skills Inventory on the following pages, and use it to inventory your skills in that story. To help you do this, I'll give you an example: the Halloween Experience. It goes like this: "*When I was seven, I decided I wanted to go out on Halloween dressed as a horse. I wanted to be the front end of the horse, and I talked a friend of mine into being the back end. But, at the last moment, he had to back out, and I was faced with the prospect of not being able to go out on Halloween. At this point, I decided to figure out some way of getting dressed up as the whole horse all by myself. I took a fruit basket, and tied some string to both sides of the basket's rim, so I could tie the basket around my rear end (bending over). This enabled me to fill out the whole horse costume by myself. I then fixed some strong thread to the horse's tail, so I could wag it by moving my hands. When Halloween came, I not only went out and had a ball; I won a prize as well.*"

Now, turn to the grid here, and see how it was filled out (in the Sample column) for this story of the Halloween Experience. The question, as you go down the skills list, is: "Did I use this skill *in this story*?" If so, color in the little box in the appropriate column on the same line as that skill.

You'll see that in the case of the Halloween Experience, the first skill listed in the grid is "assembling." You decide it wasn't used in that story; so, it remains uncolored. But the next skill, "constructing," you decide *was* used in that story; so the appropriate little square opposite it, in the Sample column, does get colored in.

Once you've gotten the hang of it, start filling in the grid using your story, Story #1, that you just wrote. The question always to ask yourself, as you go: "Did I use this skill *in this story*?" If you see a skill you know you have, and enjoy, but you didn't use it in *this* story, let that guide you in choosing your next story. Find one that shows you used that skill. You will eventually want seven stories, all told, but choose and analyze them one by one. Continue the process: write a second story, then enroll it on the grid (Story #2 using column #2) etc., until you've finished seven.

If for any reason you don't like the grid, there's an alternative list of skills on the Internet, at http://online .onetcenter.org/skills.

Once you're done with writing seven stories and enrolling them on the grid, then take a look at the completed grid. What skills *stand out*, appearing again and again, regardless of which story you told about yourself? You are looking for patterns, here.

TRANSFERABLE
SKILLS
INVENTORY

Sample: The Halloween Experience

1	2	3	4	5	6	7	Name of Skill	Example of a situation where that skill is used
							A. Using My Hands	
							1. assembling	as with kits, etc.
							2. constructing	as with carpentry, etc.
							3. or building	
							4. operating tools	as with drills, mixers, etc.
							5. or machinery	as with sewing machines, etc.
							6. or equipment	as with trucks, stationwagons, etc.
							7. showing manual or finger dexterity	as with throwing, sewing, etc.
							8. handling with precision and/or speed	as with an assembly line, etc.
							9. fixing or repairing	as with autos or mending, etc.
							10. other	
							B. Using My Body	
							11. muscular coordination	as in skiing, gymnastics, etc.
							12. being physically active	as in exercising, hiking, etc.
							13. doing outdoor activities	as in camping, etc.
							14. other	
							C. Using Words	
							15. reading	as with books; with understanding
							16. copying	as with manuscripts; skillfully
							17. writing or communicating	as with letters; interestingly
							18. talking or speaking	as on the telephone; interestingly
							19. teaching, training	as in front of groups; with animation
							20. editing	as in improving a child's sentences in an essay, etc.
							21. memory for words	as in remembering people's names, book titles, etc.
							22. other	

continued

Sample-Halloween	1	2	3	4	5	6	7	Name of Skill	Example of a situation where that skill is used
								D. Using My Senses (Eyes, Ears, Nose, Taste, or Touch)	
▨								23. observing, surveying	as in watching something with the eyes, etc.
								24. examining or inspecting	as in looking at a child's bumps, etc.
▨								25. diagnosing, determining	as in deciding if food is cooked yet
								26. showing attention to detail	as in shop, in sewing, etc.
								27. other	
								E. Using Numbers	
								28. taking inventory	as in the pantry, shop, etc.
								29. counting	as in a classroom, bureau drawers
								30. calculating, computing	as in a checkbook, arithmetic
								31. keeping financial records, bookkeeping	as with a budget, etc.
								32. managing money	as in a checking account, bank, store, etc.
								33. developing a budget	as for a family, etc.
								34. number memory	as with telephone numbers, etc.
								35. rapid manipulation of numbers	as with doing arithmetic in the head
								36. other	
								F. Using Intuition	
▨								37. showing foresight	as in planning ahead, predicting consequences, etc.
▨								38. quickly sizing up a person or situation accurately	as in everything, rather than just one or two details about them, etc.
								39. having insight	as to why people act the way they do, etc.
								40. acting on gut reactions	as in making decisions, deciding to trust someone, etc.
▨								41. ability to visualize third-dimension	as in drawings, models, blue-prints, memory for faces, etc.
								42. other	
								G. Using Analytical Thinking or Logic	
								43. researching, information gathering	as in finding out where a particular street is in a strange city
▨								44. analyzing, dissecting	as with the ingredients in a recipe, material, etc.
								45. organizing, classifying	as with laundry, etc.
▨								46. problem-solving	as with figuring out how to get to a place, etc.
								47. separating important from unimportant	as with complaints, or cleaning the attic, etc.
								48. diagnosing	as in cause and effect relations, tracing problems to their sources
								49. systematizing, putting things in order	as in laying out tools or utensils in the order you will be using them

Sample–Halloween	1	2	3	4	5	6	7	Name of Skill	Example of a situation where that skill is used
								50. comparing, perceiving similarities	as with different brands in the supermarket, etc.
								51. testing, screening	as with cooking, deciding what to wear, etc.
▨								52. reviewing, evaluating	as in looking at something you made, to see how you could have made it better, faster, etc.
								53. other	
								H. Using Originality or Creativity	
▨								54. imaginative, imagining	as in figuring out new ways to do things, or making up stories, etc.
								55. inventing, creating	as with processes, products, figures, words, etc.
▨								56. designing, developing	as with new recipes, new gadgets
								57. improvising, experiments	as in camping, when you've left some of the equipment home, etc.
								58. adapting, improving	as with something that doesn't work quite right, etc.
								59. other	
								I. Using Helpfulness	
								60. helping, being of service	as when someone is in need, etc.
								61. showing sensitivity to others' feelings	as in a heated discussion, argument
								62. listening	
								63. developing rapport	as with someone who is initially a stranger, etc.
								64. conveying warmth, caring	as with someone who is upset, ill
								65. understanding	as when someone tells how they feel, etc.
								66. drawing out people	as when someone is reluctant to talk, share
								67. offering support	as when someone is facing a difficulty alone, etc.
								68. demonstrating empathy	as in weeping with those who weep
								69. representing others' wishes accurately	as when one parent tells the other what a child of theirs wants, etc.
								70. motivating	as in getting people past hangups, and into action, etc.
								71. sharing credit, appreciation	as when working in teams, etc.
								72. raising others' self-esteem	as when you make someone feel better, less guilty, etc.
								73. healing, curing	as with physical, emotional, and spiritual ailments, etc.
								74. counseling, guiding	as when someone doesn't know what to do, etc.
								75. other	

continued

Sample – Halloween	1	2	3	4	5	6	7	Name of Skill	Example of a situation where that skill is used
								J. Using Artistic Abilities	
								76. composing music	
								77. playing (a) musical instrument(s), singing	
								78. fashioning or shaping things, materials	as in handicrafts, sculpturing, etc.
								79. dealing creatively with symbols or images	as in stained glass, jewelry, etc.
▨								80. dealing creatively with spaces, shapes, or faces	as in photography, art, architectural design, etc.
								81. dealing creatively with colors	as in painting, decorating, making clothes, etc.
								82. conveying feelings and thoughts through body, face, and/or voice tone	as in acting, public speaking, teaching, dancing, etc.
								83. conveying feelings and thoughts through drawing, paintings, etc.	as in art, etc.
								84. using words on a very high level	as in poetry, playwriting, novels
								85. other	
								K. Using Leadership, Being Up-front	
▨								86. beginning new tasks, ideas, projects	as in starting a group, initiating a clothing drive, etc.
								87. taking first move in relationships	as with stranger on bus, plane, train, etc.
								88. organizing a game at a picnic, etc.	as with a Scout troop, a team,
								89. leading, directing others	as with a field trip, cheerleading
								90. promoting change	as in a family, community, organization, etc.
▨								91. making decisions	as in places where decisions affect others, etc.
▨								92. taking risks	as in sticking up for someone in a fight, etc.
▨								93. getting up before a group, performing	as in demonstrating a product, lecturing, making people laugh, entertaining, public speaking
▨								94. selling, promoting, negotiating, persuading	as with a product, idea, materials, in a garage sale, argument, recruiting, changing someone's mind
								95. other	
								L. Using Follow-Through	
								96. using what others have developed	as in working with a kit, etc.
▨								97. following through on plans, instructions	as in picking up children on schedule
								98. attending to details	as with embroidering a design on a shirt, etc.
								99. classifying, recording, filing, retrieving	as with data, materials, letters, ideas, information, etc.
								100. other	

Pick what you guess are your top ten favorite transferable skills, and rank them in exact order. You do this by using my Prioritizing Grid, which is easy to use in its electronic form at http://tinyurl.com/cwv3wj on Beverly Ryle's site, Groundofyourownchoosing.com.

Enroll your top five favorite skills in the central petal of the Flower diagram.

Okay, once I'm all done with the Flower, and know my favorite transferable skills and favorite fields, how do I turn that into a title for my dream job?

Take a piece of paper, draw a horizontal line across the middle. Above that line, write three to five of your most favorite skills. Write them large. Below that line, write three of your most favorite fields or knowledges. Again, write them large.

Then show this paper to *everyone* you know and respect, and ask them: "What kinds of work or jobs come to mind, that would use all these skills, and most of these fields?" Get at least ten friends to make suggestions. Jot down *all* their suggestions; sift through them later to find the ones that strike home with you.

I suppose you're going to tell me, next, that I have to go out and do your famous "informational interviewing"!

Yep. That's exactly what I'm going to tell you to do. You want to explore any place that looks interesting to you, whether or not they are known to have a vacancy.

And when eventually I get invited in for an interview?

1. Get there early. Sit outside until your time has arrived. Then knock on their door.

2. In the interview, you have only one goal: to be invited back for another interview. Decisions are rarely made with only one.

3. It is important that you talk half the time, the employer talks the other half.

4. If asked a question, you should answer it in not less than 20 seconds, nor more than 2 minutes. If you still have more to say, end your two minutes with "I could say more when you want me to."

5. All questions the employer might ask fit basically into five general categories: Why are you *here*? What can you do for me? Will you help us with the problems or challenges we face here? Will you fit in with the other people here? How much are you going to cost me?

6. Keep in mind that employers like "behavioral interviewing" in many if not most cases, these days. That means, when you claim a skill, give an illustration proving you have it. If you wrote out seven stories (see page 83) this should be easy.

7. Postpone salary discussion until the very end of the interview, after they have definitely said they want you.

8. And at the very end ask *the* key question that makes all the difference as to whether you get offered the job, or not: "Given all that we've discussed, can you offer me this job?"

If you should happen to get interviews, but never get invited back, nor offered a job, check to see if you're doing something wrong. Try a site like **Checkster.com**, where individuals (like you) can invite six of your friends to anonymously evaluate you in terms of your work, as they've seen it. Maybe there's something you're unaware of, that you can fix. And, by the way, it's free.

If you keep at this, you *will* find a job, maybe even something pretty close to your dream job. Remember, the brighter your vision, the more likely you are to hit the target. The more you are *dying* to find a thing, the harder you will hunt for it.

There are jobs out there, you just have to work hard at finding them. But don't let anyone tell you that it's a waste of time to figure out what your Dream Job would be. You may come across most parts of it sooner than you think. And you will see it, because your eyes are open. You have the detailed Vision.

March, march, march toward that Vision and that goal, even if no one else appreciates what you see. Or hear. As Henry Thoreau said in Walden:

"If a man does not keep pace with his companions, perhaps it is because he hears a different drummer. Let him step to the music which he hears, however measured or far away."

9

A Plan of Action, When You're Out of Work

1. Understand there are always job vacancies out there, even if the Recession is deep. In January, 2009, 4,300,000 people in the U.S. found new jobs. 3,000,000 vacancies went unfilled. *(See chapter 1.)*

2. Understand the amount of time you're likely to be out of work. Currently, the average time to find one of the job vacancies that are out there, is over twenty weeks. You must hope it will be shorter than that. But prepare for the possibility it will be longer.

3. Understand that finding work is *your* job, not the government's.

4. Understand that you need to use more than one job-hunting method. There are 18 to choose from. That way you keep hope alive. The key to Hope is having alternatives. *(See chapters 2 & 4.)*

5. You will likely feel powerless and frustrated. To combat despair and depression, figure out some part of your life that you do have control over; and work on *that*. *Dress*. You can always dress up nicely, no matter what, while you're unemployed. You never know who you will run into, who could recommend you if you don't look skuzzy. *Gratitude*. You can always say Thanks to everyone, for anything. Your *choice, as to what area you choose*.

6. Since you likely have twenty weeks at your disposal, make your first duty to catch up on your sleep. You've got time. Don't fret if you don't sleep straight through eight hours. Normal rhythms of the human body, down through history according to studies, are three to four hours of sleep (called *first sleep*), then a couple of hours of wakefulness, followed by three to four hours of sleep again (*second sleep*). Impractical, maybe, when you're employed; very possible while you're unemployed. For further reading, see "Segmented sleep" in Wikipedia. Also: "Sleep Now, Remember Later," at http://tinyurl.com/cxoc6t.

7. Take a nap after lunch: 37% of all U.S. adults do. Twenty minutes long, three times a week, makes you 37% less likely to die of heart disease. Not practical now? "Nap time" may be a perk you can inquire about, at your next place of employment.

8. Start living very frugally, if you aren't already. Discount stores, farmer's markets, eBay, flea markets, should become your best friends. *(See chapter 3.)*

9. Find a bunch of other job-hunters that can meet regularly with you. A nice list of these, across the country, is to be found at http://tinyurl.com/7a9xbb on Susan

Joyce's great site, **job-hunt.org**. If you can't find a group, start your own. Meet at least weekly, maybe even M, W, F.

10. Hunt for new work on the Internet's job boards (or SimplyHired or Indeed, omnibus job-search engines). Use *search engines* like Google, list the word "jobs" and then *components (see chapter 7)* if job-titles don't turn up anything *(see chapter 5)*.

11. Instructions on how to write a resume are all over the Internet. Just use your search engine. Compose a nice resume, with or without help, summarizing what you want an employer to know about you, and post it on the Internet, to combat all the scattered stuff about you that a prospective employer may turn up by "Googling" you. *(See chapter 6.)*

12. If searching for your favorite job-title runs you into a brick wall, then learn how to break down a job into its most detailed parts, using your most recent job to practice on. This should be fun, if you're doing it right! *(See chapter 7.)*

13. Using this practice, then, describe the parts that make up a detailed vision of your dream job. Detailed visions enable us to hit the target, more often than not. *(See chapter 8.)*

14. If you decide you want to start your own business, go visit those who have already done the kind of thing you want to do. Pick businesses 75 miles away. Pick three. Humbly ask for their advice. What skills or knowledges do you have to have, to be successful in this line of work?

Make a list. Back home, send a thank-you note to those you interviewed. Then look at your list: check off the skills or knowledges you already have. Then figure out how you're gonna find the ones you don't have. Usually it will be a knowledge like "accounting." If so, beg, borrow, or steal an accountant, part-time or full.

15. Work hard at your job-search. 9 to 12 noon: Three hours at home in the morning, working the Internet, working on your self-inventory. 1:30 to 4:30: Three hours out visiting places, in the afternoon—places that look interesting to you from your Yellow Pages phone book, whether or not they are known to have a vacancy. Your job-finding success will be directly proportional to the hours you put in.

16. Watch what you believe. *Two cars are going down a one-way street. They are neck and neck with each other, in parallel lanes. There is a green traffic light ahead, way down at the next intersection. They both see it. They both get a thought, as they look ahead.*

One says to herself, "I'll bet that light is gonna turn red, before I reach that intersection." She doesn't slow down, but she does begin to tap the brake pedal ever so slightly. Just as she is about to reach the intersection, the light turns red. She slams on the brakes. "Aha!" she says triumphantly, "I was right!"

But the other says to herself, "I'll bet I can get across that intersection, before the light turns red." She doesn't speed up, but she does tap the accelerator pedal just a little bit. As she reaches the intersection, the light is still green. She sails across that intersection, just as the light turns red behind her. "Aha!" she says triumphantly, "I was right!"

The moral of this tale? What you believe is going to happen can help determine what actually does happen. Stay upbeat, optimistic, and as Winston Churchill famously said:

"Never never ever give up."

Index